IDAM File Organizations

Computer Science:
Distributed Database Systems, No. 15

Harold S. Stone, Ph.D., Series Editor

IBM Corporation
T.J. Watson Research Center
Yorktown, New York

Other Titles in This Series

IDAM File Organizations

by
James C. French
Vice President, Software Products
Information Solutions, Inc.
Charlottesville, Virginia

UMI RESEARCH PRESS
Ann Arbor, Michigan

Produced and distributed by
UMI Research Press
an imprint of
University Microfilms International
A Xerox Information Resources Company
Ann Arbor, Michigan 48106

Library of Congress Cataloging in Publication Data

French, James C. (James Cornelius), 1949-
  IDAM file organizations.

  (Computer science. Distributed database systems ;
no. 15)
  Revision of the author's thesis, University of
Virginia, 1982.
  Bibliography: p.
  Includes index.
  1. File organization (Computer science) 2. Electronic
data processing—Distributed processing. 3. Information
storage and retrieval systems. I. Title. II. Series.
QA76.9.F5F74 1985   001.64'2   85-1066
ISBN 0-8357-1631-7 (alk. paper)

To my family,
Katharine, Lee and Dana

Contents

List of Figures

List of Symbols

$\bar{A}_i(Q)$	Expected number of descriptors matched at level i in a D-tree
C_k^n	Binomial coefficient
$D(Q)$	Query descriptor
$D(R)$	Record descriptor
E	Encoding method
$E[\ldots]$	Expectation
$E1$	Weighted performance measure (accesses)
I	Index file
$M(t)$	Moment generating function
N	Number of records in a file
$P(z)$	Probability generating function
$Pr(\ldots)$	Probability statement
S_k^n	Stirling number of the second kind
SO	Storage overhead
a	Attribute

$\bar{a}_i(Q)$	Expected number of blocks accessed at level i in a D-tree
b	Number of records in a block
f	Number of fields in a descriptor
$\log x$	$\log_2 x$
n	Number of blocks in a file
q	Number of attributes specified in a query
r	Number of records covered by a descriptor
$\bar{s}_j(i)$	Expected number of bits set in field j in a descriptor at level i
$\bar{s}_j(r)$	Synonym for $\bar{s}_j(i)$ when r is important
$size(x)$	Size of entity x in bits
v	Attribute value
$\mathbf{w} = (w_1, \ldots, w_j)$	Descriptor format
w_j	Width of field j
$w = \sum_{j=1}^{f} w_j$	Descriptor width
$weight(x)$	Number of bits set in string x
$\nu_j = \prod_{k=1}^{j} w_k$	Volume of space defined by the first j fields
$\rho_j(i)$	Probability of matching field j at level i
$\rho_j(r)$	Synonym for $\rho_j(i)$ when r is important
$\boldsymbol{\tau} = \{\tau_1, \ldots, \tau_m\}$	Set of transforms

Preface

Over the years considerable attention has been given to the development of efficient methods for multi-attribute retrieval. The availability of extremely large commercial data bases has made this a particularly important economic issue. Many well known techniques are currently employed in high performance data base systems. This book explores a lesser known technique based on superimposed coding; this technique has its historical origins in early card filing systems, but has also been adapted for use on digital computers.

Retrieval methods based on superimposed coding abound in the literature. Indeed, considerable energy has been expended reinventing similar concepts. One goal of this book is to collect these methods together under a common umbrella, the Indexed Descriptor Access Method, or IDAM file. In this way the techniques can be treated uniformly using a common methodology. The analyses presented and the results obtained are widely applicable to many of the diverse methods subsumed by the IDAM file.

The thrust of this work is to develop a general model for retrieval techniques employing bit strings as screening mechanisms. The model is then used to analyze the behavior and storage costs of various IDAM file organizations. Performance results are derived with the analysis concentrating on the relevant parameters of the model.

The book is organized as follows. Chapter 1 presents introductory material together with a fairly detailed description of a specific instance of the technique this book investigates, the IDAM file. The formal model used in this book is introduced in chapter 2. The operation of IDAM files is described in some detail in chapter 3 along with considerations relevant to concurrent environments. Chapters 4 and 5 analyze the behavior of two particular data file organizations. The methodology used for comparing file organizations is detailed in chapter 6. In chapter 7 organizations which cluster the records of a file according to some criterion are discussed.

In a book of this sort, it is impossible to explain in detail all the necessary background material. Accordingly, some references to tutorial material have been included along with references directly relating to the material covered.

The research upon which this book is based was supported in part by a grant from the National Science Foundation (NSF Grant No. MCS80-17779). I am deeply indebted to John L. Pfaltz for his guidance during the time the research underlying this book was conducted. For all the late nights and weekends endured during the time this book was under preparation, I owe my wife Katharine its completion.

1

Introduction and Background

1.1 Introduction

This book considers the problem of file organization to support information retrieval based on the specification of one or more attributes in the data records which have been designated as keys. This problem is variously known as retrieval on secondary keys or multi-attribute retrieval. The file organizations designed to provide this capability are known as multi-attribute file organizations.

With the advent of large online data bases, the efficient solution to this problem has become increasingly important. The interactive environment imposes a variety of operational constraints among which are:

1. response time—user requests must be satisfied in a timely manner consistent with the magnitude of their requests;
2. concurrency—many users may be simultaneously anxious to query the same information; and
3. maintainability—consistent with (1) and (2) above, the file organization should be easily maintained so that performance is not badly degraded over time and maintenance operations should be possible in a concurrent environment.

Multi-attribute file organizations should therefore be evaluated with these considerations in mind.

Of particular interest is multi-attribute retrieval in large files of formatted records. Each record in a file may be accessed by means of one or more attributes (or fields). Those attributes which are actually used to access a particular set of records are called key attributes. If there is only a single key attribute it is generally called a primary key, particularly if it is known that it uniquely identifies the record. When there are several additional key attributes, they are often called secondary keys.

Access to, or retrieval of, a particular set of records is accomplished by specifying the desired values for one or more key attributes. Such accesses are also called queries. When it is known that all accesses (or queries) to a file will be by means of a single attribute, special accessing methods such as B-trees seem to be most appropriate. When the values of more than one attribute may be specified in a query, we have multi-attribute access, or as it is commonly called partial-match retrieval. Note that for a record to satisfy a multi-attribute query, the values of each of its attribute fields must match the attribute values specified in the query. It is a conjunctive query.

Normally, in partial-match retrieval we assume that at most a single value will be specified for any query attribute. If the query specifies several values that will be acceptable for a given attribute, then we have a disjunctive retrieval. More particularly, if the query specifies an interval (or range) of acceptable values for the attribute, the retrieval is called a range search.

There are many ways in which the desired attribute values may be specified in a query, or access request. The kind of format, or syntax, used is the province of data base languages. We will ignore this kind of important question and look only at the issue of efficiently implementing such queries, once they have been formulated.

An important question now arises. How does one measure the efficiency of a particular accessing method? In this book we will use the following criteria which have been widely used by many authors.

    a.   storage overhead;
    b.   computational cost expressed as the number of secondary storage accesses required to satisfy a query.

By storage overhead we mean the proportion of additional storage needed to implement the retrieval mechanism. Additional storage might be used to represent one or more index files, to represent pointers in a linked access method, or because the records may not be tightly packed in the space allocated for the data file. Storage may be measured in terms of bits, bytes, or words.

Since we are considering very large files, they are certainly represented in secondary storage. Consequently it seems reasonable to measure computational costs in terms of secondary storage accesses. Only in very special circumstances will the cost of other operations approach these access costs.

When comparing two accessing mechanisms one must be aware of the common trade-off between storage overhead and computational cost. Improvement in one is often purchased at the cost of the other. To cite two extreme examples, a simple sequential search through a file requires zero percent storage overhead, but generally at an intolerable computational cost; various fully inverted file organizations achieve better performance, but may require more storage than the data file itself. In the case of multi-attribute access there may be no optimal methodology that simultaneously minimizes both storage overhead and computational cost. One goal of the methods discussed in this book is to strike a balance between these two competing costs.

There have been many multi-attribute accessing methods proposed and/or implemented. The simplest file organization available is the sequential file where queries are evaluated by examining each record in the file. This organization is entirely appropriate in batch environments where the average number of accesses per query can be made arbitrarily small merely by accumulating large numbers of queries and satisfying them all with one pass through the data file. In an interactive environment, however, where response time is very important, this is perhaps the worst approach available except when data files are very small. A survey of several well known methods which have been proposed for the partial match retrieval problem can be found in French (1982).

There are also lesser known solutions to the multi-attribute retrieval problem based on a technique known as *superimposed coding*. A complete description of this technique has been given by Knuth (1973, vol. 3). A simple example will serve to illustrate this technique. Suppose we have a record containing two attributes whose values are represented by the 8-bit codes,

$$v_1: \ 10000011$$

and

$$v_2: \ 01010010.$$

The record is conventionally represented as the 16-bit concatention of these codes,

$$(v_1, v_2): \ 10000011 \ 01010010.$$

Using superimposed coding, the record would be represented by an 8-bit code formed by taking the logical sum or inclusive-OR of the codes for each value. In this example,

$$(v_1, v_2): \ 11010011.$$

Thus, the name of this method derives from the fact that the values of each attribute have in some way been superimposed on one another. Retrieval techniques based on superimposed coding are the topic of the next section.

1.2 Superimposed Coding Methods

According to Bourne (1963), superimposed coding was first developed and used for information storage and retrieval around 1947. Its early use was in connection with manual and mechanized edge-notched card systems. A typical example of such systems is the Zatocoding technique developed by C. N. Mooers and described by Bourne. In this system data were encoded by notching specified positions along one edge of a card. Retrieval was accomplished with the aid of long needles called tumblers which were inserted into an encoded card deck allowing a subset of the cards, those with notches in the needled positions, to drop from the deck. Subsequently, this subset of cards was manually screened for relevance by the searcher. More information about these early systems can be found in Casey and Perry (1951) and in Bourne (1963).

Since its development and use in card filing systems, superimposed coding has been used in a wide variety of applications. Bloom (1970) proposed a method of testing for set membership based on superimposed coding. In his technique, a single very large code word was kept in main memory. By testing a candidate for inclusion against the code word, his system was able to detect conclusively when a candidate was not in the set. Only after passing this test would the more expensive operations of fetching members from secondary storage and comparing them be performed.

Harrison (1971) proposed a substring test based on superimposed coding. In this system a string was represented by its set of substrings of a given length. The system involved encoding each adjacent sequence of k characters as one bit in a superimposed code word called the k-signature of the string. When a pattern match was performed, the pattern was first encoded into its k-signature which was then checked for inclusion against the k-signatures of the stored strings. Again, if inclusion was not detected, the pattern could not be contained in a string. Only after passing this test would the more expensive string pattern match be employed. This technique has been used in a conversational text editor storing 2-signatures with each line of text.

A novel variant of superimposed coding was described by Zobrist and Carlson (1977) in connection with the detection of the simultaneous occurrence of a potentially large number of prespecified values in an n-dimensional state vector. In contrast to other superimposed coding techniques, their method was based on the exclusive-OR operation and seems to be unique in that regard. As an example of the application of this technique, the authors describe a chess playing program (TYRO) which employed this method to keep track of 4,000 state tuples in its lookahead phase.

The preceding examples give some indication of the flexibility of the superimposed coding method. In the remainder of this section we will briefly survey some of the techniques for the storage and retrieval of information based on superimposed coding which have been proposed or implemented. This review is roughly in chronological order and whenever a system has actually been implemented, we will try to give some indication of its performance as well as some estimate of the storage overhead involved.

The methods proposed for storage and retrieval based on superimposed coding differ from one another chiefly in three areas:

a. the unit of information encoded—whether a superimposed code word represents a single record or a group of records;
b. the method of encoding—the way in which each of the code terms is constructed; and
c. the method of storing the code words—the organization of the resulting *code file*.

The common thread binding these methods is the use of the logical sum (inclusive-OR) to form the superimposed code word from its constituent parts.

As we have seen, the earliest application of superimposed coding was storage and retrieval from punched card files. These early systems have been analyzed by Wise (1951), who defined two major variants of superimposed coding. In the single field superimposed coding scheme, each term encoded was assigned a fixed number of positions chosen, frequently at random, from all the available positions. Multiple terms were encoded by notching each specified position. In the multiple direct coding scheme, each term was assigned a single position in a specific field of the card. An entire record was encoded by notching one position of each field on the card.

When automated systems were constructed, the only change necessary in the superimposed coding technique was in the means of representation and the mechanics of the search. Holes were replaced by zeros, notches by ones. The logical sum served as the superimposition mechanism while the needles were replaced by the logical product. Thus, the technique, involving as it does very simple binary operations, is ideally suited to implementation on digital computers.

One early hierarchical system was proposed by R. T. Moore (1961). Under this scheme a representative N-word vocabulary was chosen to describe the data. A boolean N-vector was associated with each record and constructed as follows:

1. Initially all N bit positions are set to zero.
2. For each word in the vocabulary applying to the record, a unique bit in the N-vector is set.
3. After all the applicable bits have been set, complement the N-vector to form the *rejector vector* for the record.

Note that this rejector vector now represents all the words in the vocabulary which are *not* in the associated record.

Similar rejector vectors were grouped together and organized in a tree structure. The determination of similarity and subsequent clustering of the records was based on an exhaustive search of all $2^N - 1$ possible rejector vectors coupled with a file partitioning algorithm. The underlying principle was that of maximizing the average size of blocks of records that would be rejected in a search. Because of the enormous preprocessing of the data involved, this clustering technique would only be suitable for files which retained some inherent structure well over time or those files which are essentially static in nature.

W. D. Frazer (1965) also discussed the possibility of representing a group of records by a single superimposed code word. He considered the problem of forming the logical sum of n adjacent data records (using the physical binary representation of the data records) to form an *image item* for subsequent searching. Thus, his proposal was to replace a search of $|F|$ data records by the search of a file $|F|/n$ image items, looking at the data only when a block of records emerged as possibly containing a response record. Because he used the physical representation of the data records as the item encoding method, the resultant images rapidly saturated for large n. He concluded that the optimal value of n was three or four and hence, the scheme would result in an overhead of 25–33 percent of the data file size.

A more practical system, PEEKABIT, became operational in 1963 and was described by F. C. Hutton (1968). The data file was comprised of approximately 600,000 subject index entries averaging 60 bytes (6 bits per byte) each. An 18 byte *store mask* was stored along with each record. The store mask was a specially constructed superimposed code word to facilitate rapid search. The store mask construction proceeded as follows:

1. The character code of the keywords in each entry was changed from BCD to a special 6-bit code assigning fewer bits to more frequently occurring letters.
2. A keyword mask was constructed for each keyword by first truncating the word to 18 characters if necessary. If the keyword was 6 or fewer characters in length, the keyword was placed in the mask beginning at byte 1. If longer than 6 characters, the keyword was placed in the mask beginning at byte 7 and wrapping around if necessary.
3. The store mask was the logical sum of all the keyword masks.

An example of this encoding technique is shown in figure 1.1. The octal codes shown in the figure were taken from Hutton. The resulting store mask is the logical sum of the four keyword masks.

The author claims that a test of the system showed the running time of a search to be cut in half when using the store masks as compared with the same search not using this facility. The storage overhead incurred was a fairly modest $18/60 = 30$ percent.

A very similar system was described by J. R. Files and H. D. Huskey (1969). This system differed from PEEKABIT principally in two areas: (1) the method

Figure 1.1.   Example of PEEKABIT Store Mask Encoding

	1	2	3	4	5	6	7	8	9	10	11	12	13	14	15	16	17	18
1	_	_	_	_	_	_	P	R	A	C	T	I	C	A	L	_	_	_
2	T	E	_	_	_	_	M	U	L	T	I	A	T	T	R	I	B	U
3	_	_	_	_	_	_	R	E	T	R	I	E	V	A	L	_	_	_
4	S	Y	S	T	E	M	_	_	_	_	_	_	_	_	_	_	_	_

	1	2	3	4	5	6	7	8	9	10	11	12	13	14	15	16	17	18
1	00	00	00	00	00	00	22	02	50	11	40	04	11	50	06	00	00	00
2	40	01	00	00	00	00	24	21	06	40	04	50	40	40	02	04	46	21
3	00	00	00	00	00	00	02	01	40	02	04	01	44	50	06	00	00	00
4	03	30	03	40	01	24	00	00	00	00	00	00	00	00	00	00	00	00
	43	31	03	40	01	24	26	23	56	53	44	55	55	50	06	04	46	21

used to construct the superimposed code word; and (2) the organization of the resultant code words. The data in the underlying file was similar—bibliographic text. The encoding algorithm proceeds as follows:

1. Each word in the record is screened against a Delete List to remove so-called noncontent words.
2. Each remaining word is trimmed to a pseudo-root by removing common endings.
3. The numeric values of the remaining characters are summed and this value is used to pick an integer at random from [1, *N*].
4. The corresponding bit in an *N*-bit code word is set to one.

An example of this technique is shown in figure 1.2. The numerical values were obtained by summing the character codes. The specific bit set was determined by taking the numerical value modulo 16 and adding one.

Figure 1.2.   Another Encoding Technique

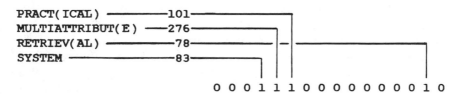

The second major difference between this system and PEEKABIT concerns the manner in which the code words were stored. Whereas in PEEKABIT each code word was stored in the data file along with the data record, here they are organized as a separate file where each entry consists of a code word and a pointer to its associated record in the data file. At the cost of a modest increase in update complexity, this organization offers the possibility that the index can be stored on a faster access device and introduces an opportunity for parallelism in the search process.

Although no hard performance results were reported, the authors argued convincingly that their method is competitive with other techniques. The reported overhead for the pilot file was a 3,000 byte index over a 100,000 byte data file, or three percent.

Files and Huskey suggested one further improvement in their index organization which was not implemented in the prototype system, but is an interesting concept. They suggested that a second level index could be formed by partitioning the code file. In their scheme, each code word would be compressed to a N/k bit code word by grouping each successive k bits in the original code word and setting the corresponding bit in the second level code word if at least one bit in the grouping was set. This second level code word determined to which of the $2^{N/k} - 1$ equivalence classes the original code word was assigned. They also observed that after constructing the second level code words, the partitioning could be accomplished by sorting.

R. A. Gustafson (1969) proposed a technique for mapping a file onto a set of lists where each record is stored on exactly one list. In his method each record having at most k keys is mapped to a w bit code word. The bit positions are chosen by a hashing function $h:A \rightarrow [1,w]$. Thus, bit positions $h(a_i)$, $i = 1,2, \ldots , k$ are set in the code word. If fewer than k bits are set by this process, ones are added at random until exactly k bits are set. The record is then stored on the list corresponding to the code word. Thus, there are C_k^w lists in the system, each associated with a unique code word. A retrieval on q attributes will require the examination of C_{k-q}^{w-q} lists. This is a very efficient system since the amount of work required decreases approximately exponentially with q.

In 1971 E. M. Cagley described a retrieval system incorporating many of the foregoing techniques. Like Frazer, Cagley considered blocks of records as the unit of encoding. The method of encoding, however, was considerably different. The approach used was essentially the multiple direct code described by Wise. In this approach, the code word for a record is broken into disjoint fields corresponding to the indexed fields of the data record. The encoding is performed on a field-by-field basis by mapping a data record value to a single bit in the corresponding field of the code word. After each record has been encoded, a *block content descriptor* is formed from the logical sum of the record descriptors. (In Cagley's system this was actually an accumulation operation done after each record was encoded.) An important property of this encoding technique is that it admits the possibility of range searching on specified fields as well as equality criteria searches.

Just as in the system of Files, et al., the code file was stored separately from the data file. However, this implementation did take advantage of the opportunity for parallelism in the retrieval software. The author describes a global processor responsible for searching the index file and a local processor responsible for analyzing a data block when one emerges as containing a possible candidate. The technique had a reported storage overhead of less than five percent of the data file size.

Cagley's method was later extended to form a hierarchical index file by aggregating descriptors in the index file. In principle, this technique can be continued indefinitely, but in practice three levels seems to give good performance. This technique, called *indexed descriptor files,* has been described by Pfaltz (1980) and has been proposed for several applications (Berman 1980, Pfaltz 1978, Pfaltz 1979). Storage estimates of 3–40 percent were reported depending mainly on how the index was constructed.

R. G. Casey (1973) proposed a tree structure very similar in spirit to the technique of Moore. Here blocks of records were grouped together and summarized by an *accumulation vector*. An accumulation vector was stored at each node of the tree and was constructed from the logical sum of all the records stored in the subtree for which the node was the root. In order to improve performance, a clustering technique based on anticipated queries was used to group records based on their response patterns. Note that performance will degrade if the types of queries change radically over the life of the file. So like Moore's technique, this method is most favorable in stable environments. Casey estimated a storage overhead of 10–30 percent and suggested that transformations might be applied to the records to combat saturation of the accumulation vectors.

A slightly different approach to the construction of superimposed index files was proposed by O. Vallarino (1976). Here a record is represented by a bit string containing one bit for every value of every attribute. A one is placed in all positions corresponding to the values the record actually has for its attributes. This results in a potentially large very sparse boolean matrix. Vallarino's proposal is to divide the matrix into submatrices and then build a *bit map* containing zeros in all positions where the corresponding submatrices are all zero and containing ones everywhere else. It can be seen that this method is an extension of the compression technique of Files and Huskey to the case of blocks of records. That is, we first imagine the vertical superimposition of some block of records followed by a horizontal compression of the code word.

C. S. Roberts (1979) describes an implementation of a partial match retrieval system which is based on single field superimposed coding. Here each value in a record is encoded into a fixed length bit string by randomly generating k bit positions in the string (where k is a parameter of the system). The logical sum of these encoded values becomes the superimposed code word for the record. These code words are stored in a separate file and Roberts estimates that query rates as high as 100 queries per second are achievable with appropriate hardware. The Suffolk County, New York telephone directory was used as a test file in an experimental system reported by the author. This directory required approximately 4.5 million bytes while the associated index required approximately .9 million bytes or 20 percent of the data file size. A typical response time of 1.5 seconds was estimated.

The only commercially available system based on superimposed coding seems to be the NDX-100 Electronic Filing Machine (Slonim et al. 1981). In this system entire documents are encoded as one or more 1024-bit code words called *surrogates*. The encoding of documents is done in hardware and thus is very fast. A worst case rate of approximately 25 queries per second for boolean queries of 64 terms through 16,000 documents was reported.

Although many variants have been explored, the systems described all rely fundamentally on one single property of superimposed coding for their viability—the power of superimposed code words to reject irrelevant records while retaining total recall. That is, each system employs a fairly inexpensive device to screen the data and thus the actual number of data records examined as possible respondents to a query is kept small. The price paid for this facility is an index with some ambiguity. This means that in any system based on superimposed coding, one has to contend with the phenomenon of *false drops*. This term originated with manual card filing schemes to describe the situation where irrelevant records (cards) dropped from the deck along with the desired records. Thus, a manual screening process was necessary to exclude these records.

1.3   Indexed Descriptor Files

The specific multi-attribute file organization investigated in this book is called the *indexed descriptor access method* or IDAM file. IDAM files encompass those multi-attribute access methods that employ descriptors arranged hierarchically in a tree structure to index data records. A particular IDAM file organization will be determined by the organization of the data file if the index is constructed from the bottom up; it will determine the organization of the data file if the index is constructed top down.

One instance of an IDAM file organization is the *indexed descriptor file* (Pfaltz, 1980). Since the operation of retrieval using this structure is illustrative of all IDAM file organizations, it will be instructive to review it here in some detail. A more detailed presentation of IDAM file organizations is given in chapter 3.

A descriptor is a string of w (for width) bits that encodes the values of the key fields of a record, or block of records. If the descriptor is formed by superimposed coding, each attribute value will set one, or more, bits among all the w possible bits. In indexed descriptor files, a descriptor is subdivided into f fields, each of width w_j, $1 \leqslant j \leqslant f$, so that

$$w = \sum_{j=1}^{f} w_j.$$

The fields need not be of the same width. Any value of attribute *j* will set precisely one of the w_j bits in field *j*. This is called *disjoint coding* by Pfaltz (1980). Thus if there are 4 key attributes, and the descriptors are of width $w = 24$, and are sub-divided into fields of width 5, 3, 9, and 7 bits respectively, a possible record descriptor $D(R)$ might be

$$D(R) = 10000\ 010\ 001000000\ 0000010.$$

The precise encoding mechanism is unimportant for this discussion, except to note that a uniform distribution of bits within each field is expected, and that this is relatively easy to attain.

A descriptor $D(\beta)$ for a block β of records is formed by simply OR-ing together all the descriptors, $D(R)$ for individual records within the block. Thus

$$D(\beta) = \bigvee_{R \in \beta} D(R),$$

where $\vee$ denotes the bitwise OR operation. A block β may consist of any number of records, subject to an upper limit imposed by the physical configuration of secondary storage.

In the access process, the block descriptor $D(\beta)$ serves as a screen. For each query Q that defines a set of desired records, a corresponding descriptor, $D(Q)$, is created. If a value v_j is specified for attribute *j* then the same bit in field *j* is set that would be set if a record descriptor were being created. If no value is specified for attribute *j*, then the corresponding field of the descriptor is set to a "don't care" condition, say of all zeros. For example, with a file whose records have descriptors as in the example above, an accessing query that specified values for attributes a_1 and a_3 might generate a query descriptor such as

$$D(Q) = 10000\ 000\ 000010000\ 0000000.$$

This query descriptor is now compared with every block descriptor $D(\beta)$ using the simple test

$$D(Q) \wedge D(\beta) = D(Q), \tag{1.1}$$

where $\wedge$ denotes the bitwise AND operation. Note that this test is equivalent to testing whether the query descriptor $D(Q)$ is contained in the block descriptor, $D(\beta)$. If test 1.1 is passed, then some record in block β *might* satisfy the query. The block β will be accessed and each of its records checked individually. But if test 1.1 fails, then no record in β can possibly satisfy the query; β need not be accessed. Descriptors screen out those portions of the file that need not be searched.

The collection of all block descriptors $D(\beta)$, together with pointers to the corresponding block of records, forms the first *index* file. To avoid exhaustively searching this entire file in a sequential manner, its records are now grouped (just block descriptors and pointers) into blocks. A descriptor for a block α in index file-1 can be formed by OR-ing all the descriptors $D(\beta)$ in the block α. If $D(Q) \wedge D(\alpha) \neq D(Q)$, then no record in any data block covered by α can possibly satisfy the query Q, so the block α in index file-1 need not be accessed or searched. The descriptors $D(\alpha)$ are collected into a second level index file-2. The records of this file may in turn be blocked, and the corresponding descriptors formed to create index file-3. Finally, an index file-h that is small enough to be resident in main memory is generated. A sequential search of this file is relatively inexpensive. (For files of fewer than a million records, three index files seem to perform satisfactorily.)

We will conclude this section with an example. A portion of an indexed descriptor file is shown in figure 1.3. The file has two index levels with each index level containing two descriptors per block. The data file has four records per block.

Figure 1.3.   Example of an Indexed Descriptor File

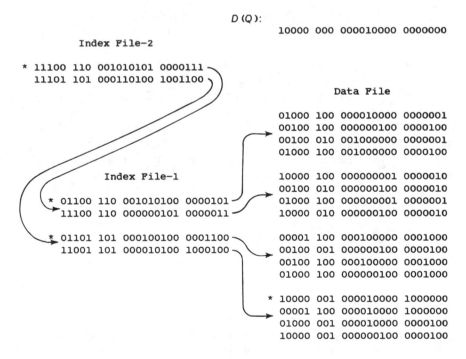

Suppose that a query Q with descriptor

$$D(Q) = 10000 \ 000 \ 000010000 \ 0000000$$

is to be processed. The blocks accessed by the search procedure to satisfy this particular query are starred in the figure. Note that $D(Q)$ matches both descriptors in index file-2. Therefore, the two blocks shown for index file-1 would have to be accessed. Now the screening process continues with only the fourth block in the data file being accessed. It can be seen that the first record in the block satisfies the query. If the file were larger, this process would continue until all matching records were found.

To summarize, when accessing a set of records specified by a query Q:

1. Create the corresponding query descriptor $D(Q)$.
2. Exhaustively compare $D(Q)$ with every descriptor in the highest level index file-h using test 1.1.
3. If test 1.1 is passed, the block β is accessed and
   a. if β is an index block, its descriptors are compared with $D(Q)$; or
   b. if β is a data block, each of its records is compared with Q.

This tree structured search process is easily implemented as a depth first search.

2

Models of Multi-attribute Retrieval

In this chapter we develop the terminology and general models used to study superimposed coding retrieval systems as described in section 1.2. We first present the data model and a more formal definition of relevant queries.

2.1 Data Model and Query Types

A *file*, F, is a collection or set of *records*, $F = \{R_1, R_2, \ldots, R_n\}$. Each record can be thought of as a list of attribute-value pairs. Let $A = \{a_1, a_2, \ldots, a_s\}$ be a set of attributes and $V = \{V_1, V_2, \ldots, V_s\}$ be the corresponding set of attribute domains. Then a record, R, is a set of pairs $R = \{(a_1, v_1), (a_2, v_2), \ldots, v_s)\}$, where $a_i \in A$ and $v_i \in V_i$. When appropriate we may also represent a record in positional notation as an s-tuple, $R = (v_1, v_2, \ldots, v_s)$. This is the familiar tuple of the relational model of data (Codd 1970).

Although in principle it is possible to retrieve records from a file based on any attribute, it is customary to designate some subset of the attributes as *key* attributes and organize the file so that retrievals involving these attributes will be efficient. This may involve the creation of an auxiliary *index*, particular storage organizations based on the key attributes, or both. Throughout this book we will assume that there are $t \leqslant s$ such attributes, but any retrieval of a specific record will return all s attributes even though t might be less than s. This assumption introduces no loss of generality in the retrieval problem and will be used later (in chapter 6) as the basis of a proposed normalized storage overhead metric.

A *query*, Q, is a request for that subset of a file, F, satisfying the query specifications. Throughout we will assume that a query Q specifies $q \leqslant t$ key attributes. We let $Q(F)$ denote the *response set* of Q, that is,

$$Q(F) = \{R \in F \mid R \text{ satisfies } Q\}.$$

The most general query is the *boolean query*, where arbitrary predicates involving the attributes of a record are allowed. The queries discussed here are special cases of general boolean queries. We are specifically interested in simple *conjunctive* queries.

A query Q is a conjunctive query if it is a specification of the form

$$Q: \text{(for all } i \in Q) \; v_{i_1} \leqslant a_i \leqslant v_{i_2}, \; v_{i_1}, v_{i_2} \in V_i. \tag{2.1}$$

The notation $i \in Q$ is intended to denote the particular q attributes specified in Q. The response set for this query is given by

$$Q(F) = \{R \in F \mid \text{(for all } i \in Q) v_{i_1} \leqslant a_i \leqslant v_{i_2}, (a_i, v_{i_k}) \in R\}.$$

When

$$v_{i_1} < v_{i_2} \text{ for some } i \in Q, \tag{2.2}$$

Q is called a *range query*. Some authors require $v_{i_1} < v_{i_2}$ for all $i \in Q$, for range queries, preferring the term *partial range query* when a range of values is not given for all the attributes specified in the query.

If (2.2) is modified so that

$$v_{i_1} = v_{i_2} \text{ for all } i \in Q, \tag{2.3}$$

and all t attributes are not specified in the query, that is, $q < t$, then Q of (2.1) is called a *partial match query*. If in addition to (2.3) above, all the attributes are specified $(q = t)$, the query is often called an *exact match query*. It should be noted that this definition of exact match query is somewhat more general than customarily found in the literature. The usual definition implies the uniqueness of a specified record. Here we allow $\mid Q(F) \mid \geqslant 1$.

In this book we are concerned with multi-attribute file organizations which support partial match queries. Throughout we will regard a partial match query, Q, on $q \leqslant t$ attributes as a specification for that subset of a file, F, satisfying the conjunction

$$(a_{i_1} = v_{i_1}) \text{ AND } (a_{i_2} = v_{i_2}) \text{ AND } \ldots \text{ AND } (a_{i_q} = v_{i_q}). \tag{2.4}$$

An exact match query is considered to be a *fully qualified* partial match query.

An important but often overlooked partial match query is the degenerate case where no attributes are specified. This *null query* requests the entire file, that is, $Q(F) = F$. It is unlikely that this kind of query would be requested in an interactive environment, but whenever a sequential scan of an entire file is required, this operation should be efficient.

Another retrieval problem often considered is *best match retrieval* (also called nearest neighbor searching). In this case, when a query is posed and $\mid Q(F) \mid = 0$, we seek to find the record(s) most similar to the desired record under some metric. The metric most commonly used is the Hamming distance (Lin, Lee and Du 1979), defined as follows:

$$\Delta(R_1,R_2) = \sum_{i=1}^{t} d(v_{1,i},v_{2,i})$$

where

$$d(x,y) = \begin{cases} 0, & x = y \\ 1, & x \neq y. \end{cases}$$

Simply expressed, this metric determines that two records are "close" if they have many attribute values in common.

Another important requirement of a multi-attribute file organization is that it have *total recall*. That is, if $Q(F)'$ is the set of records returned by a search procedure given a query Q, then $Q(F) \subseteq Q(F)'$. In essence, we will tolerate a mechanism that retrieves more records than satisfy a query, as long as it returns all the records that satisfy it.

Before examining specific retrieval techniques, we introduce a model sufficiently general to accommodate all the superimposed coding methods described earlier. As we observed, the primary differences in superimposed coding techniques arise in the encoding method used and the organization of the resultant code file, that is, in representation and structure. We will, therefore, begin by treating these areas separately and later examine their effects on one another specifically in the area of retrieval performance.

2.2   Encoding Methods

In this section we describe a generalized model of an encoding process. In the retrieval method to be examined, we will need to represent a data record by a fixed size bit string called a *record descriptor*. This section describes the construction of such descriptors.

A record descriptor is considered to be composed of *f fields*. An *encoding method*, E, is a triple $(\mathbf{w},\boldsymbol{\tau},S)$. The first component, $\mathbf{w} = (w_1,w_2, \ldots ,w_f)$, is an *f*-tuple describing the descriptor format. The w_j, $1 \leq j \leq f$, are called *field widths* and denote the number of bits assigned to each field of a descriptor. (By convention, fields are numbered left-right from one.) Thus, a descriptor has a width

$$w = \sum_{j=1}^{f} w_j.$$

The second component, $\boldsymbol{\tau} = (\tau_1,\tau_2, \ldots ,\tau_t)$, is a *t*-tuple associating a *transform* τ_k with each attribute a_k to be encoded. The specification of the τ_k can be quite arbitrary, but no value may map to zero. Finally,

$$S = \{(k_1, j_1),(k_2, j_2), \ldots ,(k_t, j_t)\}$$

is called the encoding *scheme* and associates each encoded attribute k with a specific field j in a descriptor. Given $(k, j) \in S$, we may regard τ_k as a mapping from the attribute domain into the natural numbers, $\tau_k:V_k \rightarrow \mathbf{N}$. Since $\tau_k(v_k)$ is to be encoded into field j of width w_j, τ_k can take on a maximum of $2^{w_j} - 1$ values. In practice, however, the range of τ_k will generally be more restricted.

The encoding of a descriptor can be modeled as follows. Given a record $R = (v_1,v_2, \ldots ,v_s)$ and an encoding $E = (\mathbf{w},\tau,S)$, we create the descriptor for R, denoted $D(R)$, by:

1. For each of the t attribute values, v_k, to be encoded, construct a "value descriptor" $D(v_k)$ of width w by:
   a. for $(k, j) \in S$ set field j to the binary representation of $\tau_k(v_k)$; and
   b. set all fields $i(i \neq j)$ to the value $\mathbf{0}$.
   Note: We use $\mathbf{0}$ to represent the zero vector of required length. Similarly, we will use $\mathbf{1}$ to denote the one vector when appropriate.

2. $D(R) = \overset{t}{\underset{k=1}{\mathsf{V}}} D(v_k)$. (The notation V denotes the bitwise logical sum.)

The operation in step 2 forms the final descriptor, $D(R)$, as the inclusive-OR of all the value descriptors.

The encoding process has a very simple geometric interpretation. The format $\mathbf{w}$ determines a discrete f-dimensional *bucket* space with a maximum volume of

$$\prod_{j=1}^{f} (2^{w_j} - 1)$$

points. Interpreting the descriptor fields as coordinates, the transformations τ map the file into this bucket space with each record mapping to a point.

This model will accommodate all the encoding methods described in chapter 1, but is considerably more general than is normally required. For our purposes, two special cases of the generalized encoding method will be important.

An encoding method $E = (\mathbf{w},\tau,S)$ where each attribute is represented by a distinct field in the descriptor, that is, $f = t$, so that $\mathbf{w} = (w_1,w_2, \ldots ,w_f)$, $\tau = (\tau_1, \tau_2, \ldots , \tau_f)$, with a 1-1 mapping between attributes and fields, will be called a *disjoint encoding method*. This is a generalization of the term used by Pfaltz (1980) and corresponds to the multiple direct code of Wise (1951). Simply stated, it means that each attribute of R is encoded in a separate field of $D(R)$. In this case, step 2 of the generalized encoding method can be thought of as a concatenation of the binary representations of the $\tau_k(v_k)$. Note that this is not a superimposed encoding method.

An encoding method of the form $E = (\mathbf{w}, \tau, S)$ where $\mathbf{w} = (w_1)$, $\tau = (\tau_1, \tau_2, \ldots, \tau_t)$ and $S = \{(1,1),(2,1), \ldots, (t,1)\}$ is called a *single field superimposed encoding method*. Thus, a record descriptor is a single field of $w = w_1$ bits and all t attributes are mapped to it.

By the *weight* of a bit string x, denoted *weight* (x), we mean the number of ones in the bit string. A transform τ is a weight-k transform if *weight* $(\tau(v)) = k$ for all $v \in V$. Hence a weight-k transform can create at most $C_k^{w_j}$ unique bit patterns or code words in some field j.

Thus far we have said nothing specific about the nature of the transformations τ except that they must map into a finite subset of the positive integers. As we will see, retrieval performance is influenced strongly by the average number of ones occurring in descriptors.

The ambiguity associated with superimposed coding methods results when the apparent existence of a value is synthesized by the encoding scheme. This is best demonstrated by means of an example. Suppose that a single field superimposed encoding method is used to encode records containing two attributes. Let the descriptor be of width $w = 4$ and $\tau_1 = \tau_2 = \tau$. Assume that the transform τ selects two bit positions at random from the four available positions. Therefore, the code words must come from the set $\{1100, 0110, 0011, 1001, 1010, 0101\}$. Consider a record $R = \{(a_1, v_1),(a_2, v_2)\}$ with $\tau(v_1) = 1100$ and $\tau(v_2) = 0110$. This record will have the descriptor $D(R) = 1110$. Notice that the query descriptor $D(Q) = 1010$ will match this record descriptor and thus, the record appears to have the requested attribute. Although this example is unrealistically small, it does serve to illustrate the problem of false drops that occur when a retrieval mechanism accesses records which initially appear to satisfy a query, but in fact do not.

Two dominant factors influencing the choice of an encoding method are: (1) the variety of queries possible under the method; and (2) the retrieval performance desired. Performance considerations are deferred until chapter 6. In the next section we look briefly at the types of queries possible using descriptors.

2.3 Retrieval Using Descriptors

We have seen that a partial match query Q is a specification of the form

$$(a_{i_1} = v_{i_1}) \text{ AND } (a_{i_2} = v_{i_2}) \text{ AND } \ldots \text{ AND } (a_{i_q} = v_{i_q}).$$

Let $I = \{D(R) \mid R \in F\}$ be the set of record descriptors formed by encoding a file F. To be precise, I is a multiset since record descriptors need not be unique, but we will assume that the correspondence between each record and its descriptor is implicitly maintained so that each element of I is unique. We will call I an *index file* over the file F.

To retrieve the set of records specified by Q, the query is first encoded in the same way the records were encoded to yield $D(Q)$ a *query descriptor*. (Note here than any unspecified fields in the query descriptor are set to 0 in $D(Q)$.) The query descriptor is then compared against all the record descriptors $D(R) \in I$ in the index file using the simple screening criterion

$$D(Q) \wedge D(R) = D(Q) \tag{2.5}$$

where $\wedge$ denotes the bitwise logical product. Since the unspecified fields in $D(Q)$ have been set to 0, test (2.5) will be true if and only if every bit set in $D(Q)$ is also set in $D(R)$. This screening process will create a set of candidate records denoted $Q(I)$ where

$$Q(I) = \{R \in F \mid D(Q) \wedge D(R) = D(Q)\}.$$

Finally the response set $Q(F)$ is constructed as follows,

$$Q(F) = \{R \in Q(I) \mid (a_{i_1} = v_{i_1}) \text{ AND } (a_{i_2} = v_{i_2})$$
$$\text{AND} \ldots \text{AND} (a_{i_q} = v_{i_q})\}. \tag{2.6}$$

Thus the final determination of inclusion in the response set is always based on an appeal to the actual query values, but now this test is only necessary on a smaller portion of the file since presumably $\mid Q(I) \mid \ll \mid F \mid$.

Recall that we originally defined $Q(F)$ as $Q(F) = \{R \in F \mid R \text{ satisfies } Q\}$. Thus in (2.6) we have implicitly assumed that $\{R \in F \mid R \text{ satisfies } Q\} \subseteq Q(I)$. We will have more to say about this assumption in the next section.

The retrieval steps just outlined form a general model of descriptor based access and retrieval that encompasses both superimposed and disjoint encoding schemes. However, in the remainder of this book we will concentrate on the latter. The following discussion will explain why disjoint encoding schemes are generally preferable to superimposed schemes when encoding formatted files. Let Q be the query $(a_1 = v_1)$ AND $(a_2 = v_2)$, where $V_1 = V_2$ and $v_1 \neq v_2$. We are asking here for two separate values of two different attributes with the same underlying domain. Let I and I' denote the index files over F constructed according to a disjoint and single field method, respectively.

Suppose that these indexes are constructed using the transforms $\tau_1 = \tau_2 = \tau$ and $\tau'_1 = \tau'_2 = \tau'$, respectively. The query descriptors for each method are given by $D(Q) = \tau(v_1) \mid\mid \tau(v_2)$ and $D(Q)' = \tau'(v_1) \vee \tau'(v_2)$. (The notation $\mid\mid$ denotes the concatenation of specified values.) Now consider a typical record $R = \{(a_1, x_1),(a_2, x_2)\}$ in the file. Under each encoding the resulting record descriptors are $D(R) = \tau(x_1) \mid\mid \tau(x_2)$ and $D(R)' = \tau'(x_1) \vee \tau'(x_2)$. Now when text (2.5) is applied, we have

$$D(Q) \wedge D(R) = \tau(v_1) \wedge \tau(x_1) \mid\mid \tau(v_2) \wedge \tau(x_2) \qquad (2.7)$$

and

$$D(Q)' \wedge D(R)' = (\tau'(v_1) \vee \tau'(v_2)) \wedge (\tau'(x_1) \vee \tau'(x_2)). \qquad (2.8)$$

Consider the files $Q(I)$ and $Q(I')$. It can be seen from (2.7) that $Q(I)$ will contain only those records in F that can possibly satisfy Q. However, notice from (2.8) that $Q(I')$ will contain records that can satisfy the query $(a_1 = v_2)$ AND $(a_2 = v_1)$, as well as those records possibly satisfying Q. Although $Q(F) \subseteq Q(I)$ and $Q(F) \subseteq Q(I')$, potentially $\mid Q(I') \mid \gg \mid Q(I) \mid$ leading to reduced performance. This situation arises because single field encoding cannot distinguish attributes. While this may be acceptable in some cases, (indeed, it is sometimes desirable; e.g., text encoding), it is particularly undesirable for formatted records of the type occurring frequently in business and other applications. This potential decrease in performance is reason enough to choose a disjoint encoding method, but there are also other reasons which will become clear in the next section. In addition there are some advantages inherent in disjoint encoding methods particularly with respect to the kinds of queries one can pose directly.

Although we are specifically interested in the partial match retrieval problem, we digress briefly to demonstrate the flexibility of descriptors to express other more general queries. This discussion is not intended to be exhaustive, but merely suggestive of the query possibilities available. The suggested extensions in the remainder of this section assume a disjoint encoding method.

To begin, we will alter slightly the test criterion used for screening descriptors. Returning to the geometric interpretation of an encoding process, we imagine a query descriptor as describing a set of points and change our screening criterion to determine whether a record descriptor (point) is in the set. In order to achieve this representation, we let the specified fields of $D(Q)$ be formed as before, but now the unspecified fields of $D(Q)$ are all set to $\mathbf{1}$. Symbolically the selection criterion becomes $D(R) \cap D(Q) \neq \varnothing$. Algorithmically this test can be expressed as $D_j(R) \wedge D_j(Q) \neq \mathbf{0}, j = 1, 2, \ldots, f$ where the notation $D_j(X)$ denotes the jth field of the descriptor X.

The price paid for this more general test is that the screening criterion now must be performed on a field-by-field basis whereas the original test could be conducted on the descriptor as a whole. We now describe some extensions possible with this new test.

If we regard the partial match query as an interfield conjunction, we might ask what intrafield operations are possible.

Intrafield Disjunctions

By an intrafield disjunction we mean a query of the form

$$(a_i = v_{i_1}) \text{ OR } (a_i = v_{i_2}) \text{ OR } \ldots \text{ OR } (a_i = v_{i_p})$$

for some attribute a_i with domain V_i and $v_{i_k} \in V_i$, for $k = 1, 2, \ldots, p$.

The appropriate query descriptor will have $\tau_i(v_{i_1}) \lor \tau_i(v_{i_2}) \lor \ldots \lor \tau_i(v_{i_p})$ mapped to field j for $(i, j) \in S$.

Range Searching

A range criterion is a statement of the form $(v_{i_1} \leqslant a_i \leqslant v_{i_2})$, $v_{i_1}, v_{i_2} \in V_i$ for some attribute a_i. This is just a special case of an intrafield disjunction. If we make use of an order preserving transformation, one for which $v_{i_1} \leqslant v_{i_2}$ implies $\tau(v_{i_1}) \leqslant \tau(v_{i_2})$, then we merely set all bits in the field from $\tau(v_{i_1})$ to $\tau(v_{i_2})$. One type of order preserving transformation discussed by Cagley (1971), which is useful when the domain of a_i is large, is to divide the domain into approximately equifrequent intervals and then map each interval to a single bit in the field.

Negation

It is possible to define negation meaningfully in a limited number of cases. In order to negate a field j the following conditions must be met:

1. $(p,r),(q,r) \in S$ implies $p = q$. That is, only one attribute maps to the field; and
2. τ_j is 1-1 and weight-1.

When these conditions hold we can make statements of the form $(a_i \neq v_i)$ and generate the field as $\neg \, \tau_i(v_i)$. Similarly we may define an intrafield conjunction such as

$$(a_i \neq v_{i_1}) \text{ AND } (a_i \neq v_{i_2}), \quad v_{i_1}, v_{i_2} \in V_i$$

and by DeMorgans's law the field in the query descriptor is set to $\neg \, (\tau(u) \lor \tau(v))$.

Interfield Disjunction

If two fields satisfy the conditions for negation then it is possibly to specify interfield disjunctions of the form $(a_1 = v_1)$ OR $(a_2 = v_2)$, $v_1 \in V_1$, $v_2 \in V_2$, which by DeMorgan's law can be stated in the query descriptor as $\neg \, [\, \neg \, \tau_1(v_1) \land \neg \, \tau_2(v_2)]$. Note, however, that in this case it would be necessary to use the query descriptor $\neg \, \tau_1(v_1) \land \neg \, \tau_2(v_2)$ to specify the set of points (records) *not* relevant and the screening criterion must be altered to accept a point not in the set, that is, exclude points in the set.

These examples serve to illustrate the potential of descriptors to support a flexible query language. In the next section we introduce the model for organizing descriptors into index files.

2.4 Index Organization

We have seen how descriptors for a file of data records can be constructed and used to perform retrievals. Throughout we have assumed that the record descriptors were stored in a sequential file and screened individually against a test criterion. We now introduce a hierarchical model for the storage of record descriptors.

Given a file F of records and an encoding method E, let $I_0 = \{D(R) \mid R \in F\}$ be an index file over F. For an arbitrary partial match query Q define

$$Q(I_0) = \{R \in F \mid D(Q) \wedge D(R) = D(Q)\}.$$

Recall that the response set for Q is given by $Q(F) = \{R \in F \mid R \text{ satisfies } Q\}$. An index file I is called *complete* if for all Q, $Q(F) \subseteq Q(I)$. Clearly, I_0 is a complete index file over F. The concept of completeness needs some further explanation.

Suppose we have a file F and create an index, $I(F)$ over F by some process ϕ that is $\phi:F \rightarrow I(F)$. The index consists of a set of entries $I(F) = \{\phi(R) \mid R \in F\}$. Given a query Q, let

$$A(Q, F) = \{R \in F \mid R \text{ satisfies } Q\}$$

denote the answer. Here $A(Q,F)$ may be regarded as the set of records one would find by sequentially scanning F and applying Q to each record $R \in F$.

Now to search the index, we assume that the original query Q is transformed by ϕ into an appropriate test criterion, $\phi(Q)$, applicable to the index entries. Let $B_I(Q,F)$ denote the set of index entries satisfying this new criterion. That is,

$$B_I(Q,F) = \{\phi(R) \in I(F) \mid \phi(R) \text{ satisfies } \phi(Q)\}.$$

After identifying the relevant index entries, we now extract the set of records associated with these entries. Denoting this set of candidate records by $C_I(Q,F)$, we have

$$C_I(Q,F) = \{R \in F \mid \phi(R) \in B_I(Q,F)\}.$$

Finally, to arrive at the response set, the candidate records are screened against Q. This results in the set $A_I(Q,F)$ given by

$$A_I(Q,F) = \{R \in C_I(Q,F) \mid R \text{ satisfies } Q\}.$$

Using this notation, we say that an index $I(F)$ over a file F is complete if and only if for all Q,

$$A_I(Q,F) = A(Q,F).$$

Simply stated, an index is complete if the response set derived from the index is the desired answer to the query. This definition implies that $A(Q,F) \subseteq C_I(Q,F)$, which just says that all the desired records are contained in the set of records identified by the index as candidates.

Although this discussion applies equally well to indexed file structure, we are concerned here with its application to files of descriptors. In this context, ϕ can be regarded as the encoding method E. Then an index entry, $\phi(R)$ can be thought of as the descriptor-pointer pair

$$\phi(R) = \left[D(R), ptr(R) \right].$$

Throughout we will tacitly assume that $ptr(R)$ exists either explicitly or implicitly and abbreviate the notation to $\phi(R) = D(R)$.

Since ϕ under this interpretation is the encoding method, $\phi(Q)$ is just $D(Q)$. Hence, the statement "$\phi(R)$ satisfies $\phi(Q)$" can be replaced by "$D(Q) \wedge D(R) = D(Q)$", the screening criterion.

We will continue to use the simplified notation

$$Q(F) = \{R \in F \mid R \text{ satisfies } Q\} \equiv A(Q,F)$$

and

$$Q(I) = \{R \in F \mid D(Q) \wedge D(R) = D(Q)\} \equiv C_I(Q,F)$$

to denote the response set and the set of candidate records identified by the index respectively. When it is known that the index I is complete, the response set can also be expressed as

$$Q(F) = \{R \in Q(I) \mid R \text{ satisfies } Q\}.$$

The property of completeness is very important to the construction of "correct" index files. It can be seen to be a necessary and sufficient condition to guarantee that all desired records will be retrieved for every query. It is not, however, a very strong condition. To see this, note that the trivial index $I = \{1\}$ is complete since $Q(I) = F$ and $Q(F) \subseteq F$, implies that $Q(F) \subseteq Q(I)$. Nevertheless, any algorithm creating index files must guarantee completeness and any algorithm manipulating index files must preserve completeness.

We are now ready to introduce the hierarchical model for the storage of record descriptors. Suppose we partition I_0 arbitrarily into subsets $B_{0,k}$:

$$I_0 = B_{0,1} \cap B_{0,2} \cap \ldots \cap B_{0,n_0}.$$

Each $B_{0,k}$ is a set of descriptors, so we can define $D(B_{0,k})$ to be the logical sum of all the descriptors in $B_{0,k}$. Now form the set I_1:

$$I_0 = \left\{ D_{1,k} \mid D_{1,k} = \vee D_{0,k}, \, D_{0,k} \in B_{0,k} \right\}.$$

To clarify this notation, note that $D_{i,k} \in I_i$ is a descriptor at level i and moreover $D_{i,k} = D(B_{i-1,k})$. Because each descriptor in I_1 is formed by OR-ing descriptors in I_0, I_1 is a complete index over F with $|I_1| = n_0$. The following general procedure can be used to construct a complete index file I_{i+1} from an index I_i:

1. Partition I_i arbitrarily, $I_i = B_{i,1} \cap B_{i,2} \cap \ldots \cap B_{i,n_i}$.

2. Form I_{i+1} as $I_{i+1} = \left\{ D_{i+1,k} \mid D_{i+1,k} = \vee D_{i,k}, \, D_{i,k} \in B_{i,k} \right\}$.

Note that $|I_{i+1}| = n_i$.

This process can be continued. At each step a file of descriptors is partitioned and a new file is created by OR-ing the descriptors in each subset. Note that this is equivalent to representing subsets of the file by superimposed code words.

Theorem 2.1: If I_i is a complete index over a file F and I_{i+1} is constructed by the above procedure, then I_{i+1} is a complete index over F. That is, $Q(F) \subseteq Q(I_{i+1})$ for all Q.

Proof: For any Q consider $R \in F$ such that $R \in Q(F)$. Since I_i is complete, $R \in Q(I_i)$. It will be sufficient to show that $R \in Q(I_i)$ implies $R \in Q(I_{i+1})$.

Let $D(R)$ denote the descriptor for R. Now $R \in Q(I_i)$ implies that

$$D(R) \wedge D_i = D(R) \tag{2.9}$$

for some $D_i \in I_i$. By the procedure, there exists some $D_{i+1} \in I_{i+1}$ such that

$$D_{i+1} = D_i \vee \{\text{other descriptors in } I_i\},$$

so that $D_i \wedge D_{i+1} = D_i$. This implies that

$$D(R) \wedge (D_i \wedge D_{i+1}) = D(R) \wedge D_i,$$

which from (2.9) can be rewritten as $D(R) \wedge D_{i+1} = D(R)$. Therefore $R \in Q(I_{i+1})$ for all $R \in Q(I_i)$ and hence, $Q(I_i) \subseteq Q(I_{i+1})$. But since $Q(F) \subseteq Q(I_i)$, it follows that $Q(F) \subseteq Q(I_{i+1})$ and thus, I_{i+1} is complete. $\square$

The following obvious but useful result follows immediately.

Corollary 2.1.1: An index I constructed by any means which can be modeled by the above procedure is complete.

A collection of h index files $I_0, I_1, \ldots, I_{h-1}$ generated by the above procedure can be viewed in two ways. First, as we have already seen each I_i is a complete index for F. An alternate view is that I_i is an index for I_{i-1}. This view leads to a hierarchical index structure where each level is a successively coarser index over F. As an imperfect analogy, we could consider the coarsest index as specifying

Figure 2.1.   Tree Representation of Index Files

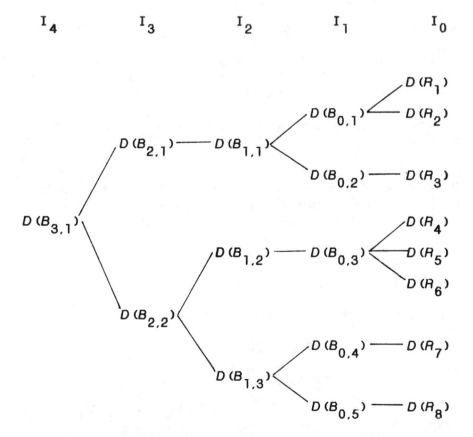

one or more volumes of a set of books. The next level might narrow the search to chapters. Subsequent levels might further reduce the scope of a search to sections, pages, paragraphs etc.

We can always represent this structure as a forest (containing a single tree whenever $|I_{h-1}| = 1$) of trees of height h. If we add the file I_h which is the logical sum of all the descriptors in I_{h-1}, a single rooted tree is guaranteed. This can be represented graphically as in the example of figure 2.1. Note that we are using the term *level* in its accepted sense, but are numbering them from bottom to top (i.e., leaves are at level 0).

Since each node in the tree is the logical sum of its immediate successors, it would be convenient to have these successors physically adjacent in a data structure in order to facilitate this operation. An appropriate data structure is the "Knuth transform" of the tree (Pfaltz 1977). In this representation (see figure 2.2) the successors of a node are all logically contiguous.

Figure 2.2. Knuth Transform of Tree of Figure 2.1

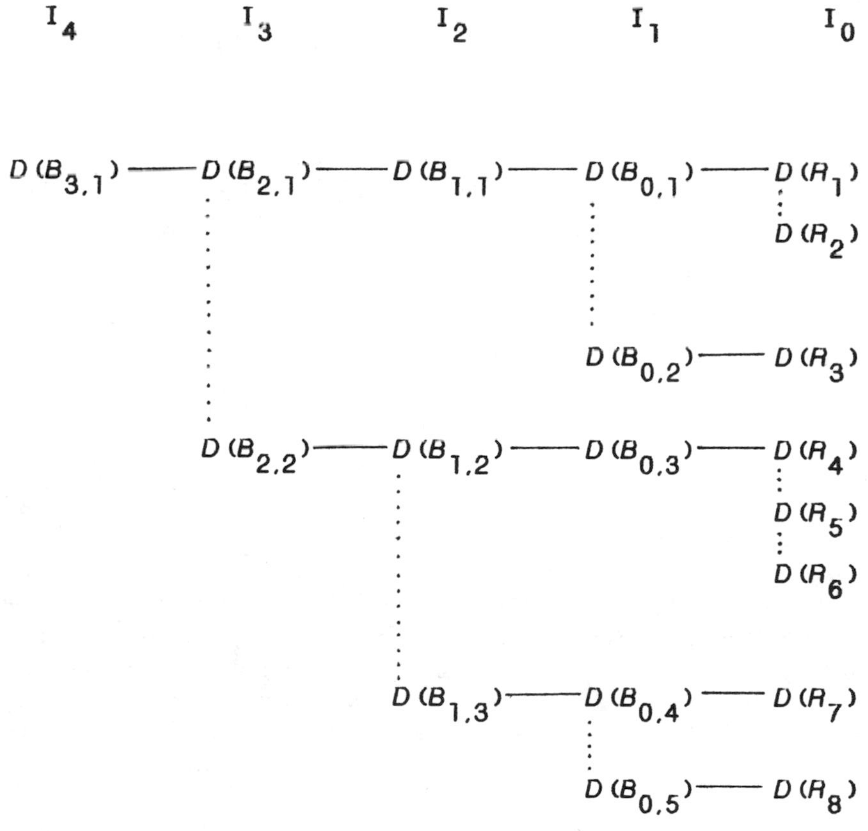

As a final refinement, we require all the immediate successors of a node to be physically contiguous and store them in a *block*. Each block is back linked to its parent and all the blocks at any level are made logically contiguous (see figure 2.3). We call this data structure a *D*-tree.

Figure 2.3.   Index Files as a *D*-tree

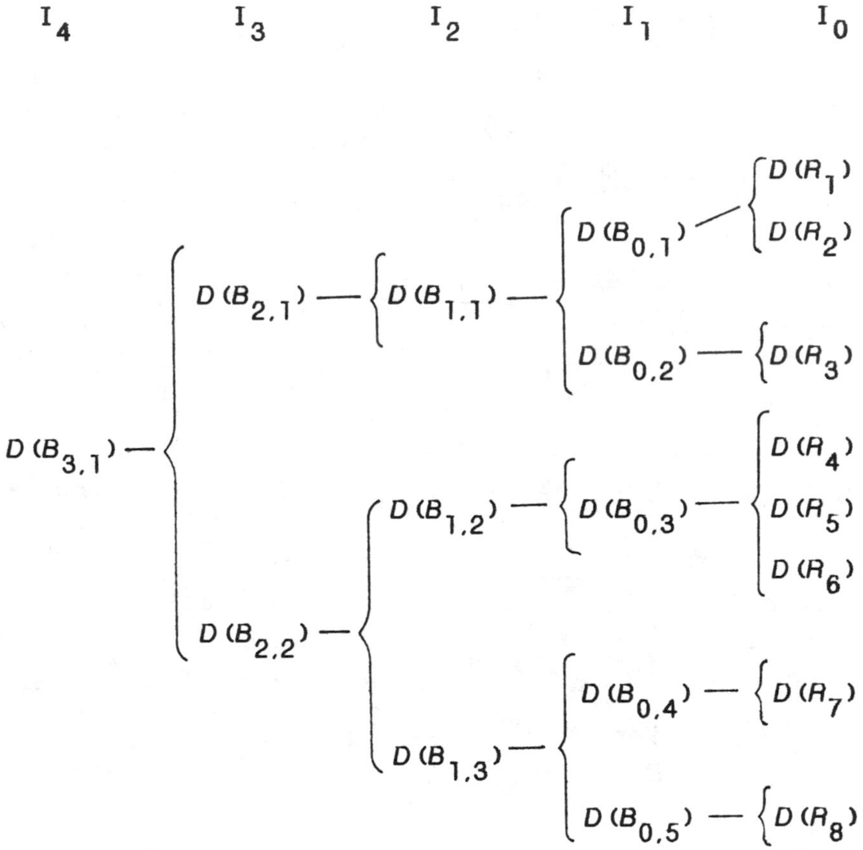

$$I_4 \qquad I_3 \qquad I_2 \qquad I_1 \qquad I_0$$

Each level of a *D*-tree can be regarded logically as a blocked sequential file. Note that the index structure is independent of the encoding method, although the retrieval performance is greatly influenced by both the encoding and the structure.

Each descriptor in a *D*-tree is the root of some subtree containing a portion of the data file F in its leaves. When there are r records in the leaves of a subtree for which a descriptor $D(B_{i,k})$ is the root, we say that $D(B_{i,k})$ *covers* r data records.

It is clear from the construction of D-trees that the number of bits set in a descriptor at any level will depend only on the encoding method used and the number of records recovered by the descriptor. Since the inclusive-OR operation is associative and commutative, the ordering of the records covered by a descriptor will not affect the number of bits set.

We conclude this section with one final observation. It is not possible in general to determine the number of successors of a descriptor $D(B_{i,k})$ from knowledge of $D(B_{i,k})$ alone. Hence, if this information is important, it must be maintained separately or stored in the D-tree along with the descriptors.

3

The Indexed Descriptor Access Method

In this chapter we introduce a file organization for partial match retrieval. Procedures for manipulating this structure are described along with implementation considerations.

3.1. IDAM Files

The particular file organization we will investigate is a straightforward application of D-trees to the partial match retrieval problem. If we are given a file F and an encoding method E, we can construct (by any means consistent with the model outlined in section 2.4) a D-tree over F. For example, define I_1 to be

$$I_1 = \{D(B_{0,k}) \mid D(B_{0,k}) = \bigvee_{R \in B_{0,k}} D(R), \; k = 1, 2, \ldots, n_0\}$$

where $F = B_{0,1} \cap B_{0,2} \cap \ldots \cap B_{0,n_0}$ is the data file. Thus, each descriptor in I_1 points to a subset of data records rather than individual record descriptors. Now using the partitioning procedure outlined in section 2.4, we can create the index files $I_2, \ldots, I_h$.

We call this file organization an IDAM file for indexed descriptor access method. The term IDAM was originally used to denote a variant of the indexed descriptor files of Pfaltz, Berman and Cagley (1980) prototyped for the Federal Judicial Center (Berman 1980). It is used here to denote any multi-attribute file organization based on D-trees.

The physical realization of an IDAM file is an extended D-tree structure. Here each level of the tree is logically considered to be just a blocked sequential file. While we have made a careful distinction between F, a file of data records, and the I_i, files of index entries, there is no real need to do this. We can simply let

$$F_i = \{B_{i,k}, k = 1, 2, \ldots, n_i\}, \; i = 0, 1, \ldots, h - 1,$$

where F_0 denotes F the data file and F_i, $i > 0$, denotes some index file. This notational change will make the subsequent discussion a bit easier and clearer.

Each file F_i consists of n_i blocks containing at most b_i entries per block. (The b_i are called *blocking factors*.) Here the neutral term entry will be used when it is unnecessary to distinguish between data records and descriptors as components of a particular file. We call the $B_{0,k}$ *data blocks* and the $B_{i,k}$ ($i > 0$) *index blocks*.

Each file F_i contains N_i entries and $N_0 = N$ the data file size. As a mnemonic device for remembering these conventions note that $n_i \leqslant N_i$, that is, the number of blocks is typically smaller than the number of records in a file. Thus, small n for blocks; large N for records. When each block in a file F_i is fully packed, the number of blocks is given by

$$n_i = \frac{N_i}{b_i}.$$

This conceptual change has not introduced any loss of generality in the possible *D*-trees over *F*. To see this, note that we can always make $b_0 = 1$ and hence, $F_1 = I_0$ of the last chapter. In this case, the data file can be considered to be appended to the *D*-tree rather than replacing an index level.

One important benefit obtained from this approach is that the data file can be organized in any conventional fashion (sequential, hashed, etc.) as long as each block of the file $B_{0,k}$ is addressable. In this way, the index and the data file can remain logically separate entities.

We can characterize an IDAM file as a *D*-tree of height *h* over a data file *F*. This structure may be regarded as a tree with the following properties:

1. level *h* is the "root";
2. all records occur in the leaves;
3. all paths from the root to the leaves have the same length *h*;
4. non-leaf nodes at level *i* contain descriptors for nodes at level $i - 1$; and
5. each node at level $i > 0$ contains at most b_i descriptors.

Another useful property of IDAM files follows from the completeness of the index files. Any level *i* may serve as the root of the tree, or more accurately forest. This property can be exploited to improve retrieval performance in some cases. This issue is considered further in section 4.1.

The minimal structure of index and data blocks is shown in figure 3.1. This structure is considered minimal since it may be desirable to include more information in each block, but at least this much is necessary. Figure 3.2 illustrates the structure of an IDAM file. Here level 0 is the data file and each higher level is an index file. Note also that each level is provided with a separate entry point.

3.2 Operations on IDAM Files

In this section we discuss the ordinary file operations on IDAM files: retrieval, creation, insertion, deletion, and update.

Figure 3.1. Minimal Format for Index and Data Blocks

Index Block:

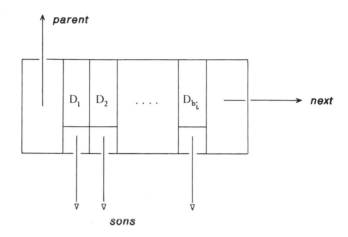

Data Block:

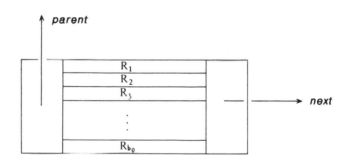

Retrieval

To perform a partial match retrieval on an IDAM file we simply perform an exhaustive depth first search on the file. A query Q is first encoded to get $D(Q)$. This query descriptor is then compared against all the descriptors in the highest index level. Whenever a match occurs, the corresponding block at the next level is fetched and examined. Finally, when a data block is encountered, the query values are compared against the actual data values stored in the records. This process is summarized by the procedure *DFS* in figure 3.3.

Figure 3.2.   Structure of an IDAM File

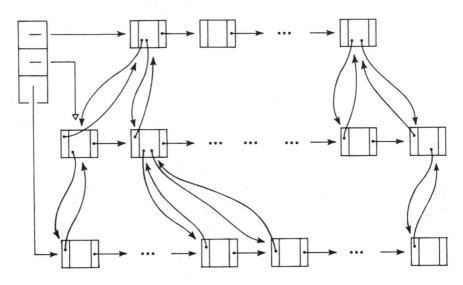

Figure 3.3.   *D*-tree Retrieval Algorithm

procedure $DFS\ (Q, level)$

    procedure $search\ (block, level)$
    begin
       if $level \neq 0$ then
          foreach D in $block$ do
            if $D(Q) \wedge D = D(Q)$ then
               $search\ (son\_of\ (D), level-1)$;
       else
          foreach R in $block$ do
            if *attributes in R match attributes in* Q then
               $add\_to\_response\_set\ (R)$;
      end;

begin
    foreach B in $F[level]$ do
      $search(B, level)$;
end;

Notice that procedure *DFS* is independent of the tree structure and will work correctly on any IDAM file. Another important observation is that *DFS* will work correctly beginning at any level. The call *DFS(Q,h)* will initiate a complete depth first search while the call *DFS(Q,0)* will initiate a sequential search of the data file.

Creation

The philosophies governing the creation of IDAM files can be grouped broadly into two categories: bottom up methods and top down methods. These methods differ in one fundamental aspect: whether the index is used to determine the placement of the records within the file, or simply reflects the placement determined by other means. In the bottom up methods, the records are first placed in the data file and then the index is updated to reflect the additions. In the top down methods, the index is consulted during record insertion in an effort to find a "best" location for each record. This is done primarily to influence retrieval performance.

Insertion

The insertion of records into an IDAM file can be thought of as two separate and distinct phases. First, a decision must be made as to which block in the data file a record is to be stored in. In the event that no block is found to be suitable, a new block must be created. This is essentially a policy decision and will completely determine the structure of the IDAM file. The second phase is completely mechanical and involves the actual manipulation of the file structure. It is in this phase that the record will be physically placed into the file and the index adjusted accordingly.

To update the index the new descriptor is OR-ed into the parent descriptor of each block along the access path. Note that this process may be stopped if containment in a parent descriptor is detected. The operation of updating the index may be complicated by the need to create new index blocks or entire paths in the tree.

Deletion

To delete a record from an IDAM file, a retrieval must first be performed to ascertain the existence of the record and to locate it in the data file. When the record has been located, it can be deleted as appropriate to the data file organization.

Two strategies are available for updating the index. In the first, the block descriptor is recomputed from the remaining records. This new descriptor replaces the parent and the descriptor of the block containing the parent is recomputed. This process is repeated until the record access path has been updated. It should be noted that the recomputation of the descriptors along the access path *must* use the inclusive-OR operation to guarantee the completeness of the resultant index. An operation such as the exclusive-OR to remove the deleted descriptor from a block descriptor would in many cases remove too many bits from the block descriptor. Indeed, it would be possible with this operation to leave a field in the descriptor empty.

The second strategy is to leave the index alone. This approach would still leave the index complete, but will have the effect after many deletions of degrading the retrieval performance. However, in relatively stable environments this approach would be appropriate. The file can be rebuilt at regular intervals to keep the performance from becoming too poor.

Update

When updating an IDAM file, the important consideration is whether any indexed attributes are affected by the update. When no indexed attributes are involved the update can proceed with no effect on the index. When indexed attributes are the target of the update, care must be taken to ensure the completeness of the index after the update has processed. This can be accomplished in two ways. First, the update can be applied to the data record, a new record descriptor formed for the record, and the record access path updated to reflect the new descriptor. Alternatively, the update can be treated as a delete/insert pair and handled as described earlier.

3.3   Concurrency and IDAM Files

The discussion of the operations described in section 3.2 assumed a single user environment. In this section we will develop a multiuser synchronization mechanism, *combination locks,* to facilitate the access of IDAM files in concurrent environments.

The goal of concurrency in a computing system is to improve the overall system performance (generally measured as response time) by more fully utilizing the available system resources. In this section we consider concurrent access of an important subset of these system resources—the file system. We begin with a brief review of the terminology associated with this subject. A short introduction can be found in Date (1977) or Wiederhold (1977).

When users access the information in a data base, they expect the information stored there to be consistent. Informally, consistency means that the data satisfy certain outside integrity constraints. As an example, consider a concert ticket agent's data base. Suppose that the information

$$(seat\_holder,\ seat\_number)$$

and

$$(concert\_name,\ total\_seats,\ seats\_sold)$$

is stored in the data base. At any time, the various agents using the system will assume that

1. no two seat holders have the same seat number; and
2. for any concert, *seats__available* = *total__seats* − *seats__sold*.

A more thorough treatment of consistency can be found in Eswaran et al. (1976).

The processes operating on the file system are customarily called *transactions*. Transactions are composed of atomic units known as *actions*. It is assumed that each transaction when viewed alone starts with a consistent data base and leaves a consistent data base when it terminates.

Although transactions preserve consistency, it is possible for the data base to become temporarily inconsistent during the execution of a transaction. Again consider the ticket agent example. Suppose an agent is selling a seat. We may assume that this transaction proceeds in two steps:

1. assign a seat number to the customer; and
2. update the number of seats sold.

After the first step has completed but before the second step has begun, the data base will clearly be in an inconsistent state. This transaction can be expressed as the following sequence of actions.

T: 1.   read *seat__number*
        2.   write *seat__holder, seat__number*
        3.   read *seats__sold*
        4.   increment *seats__sold*
        5.   write *seats__sold*

The second step of the transaction is represented by actions 3–5.

To process multiple transactions concurrently, it is necessary to interleave their actions while guaranteeing the consistency of the data base. If the transactions do not conflict, this process is trivial. (Two transactions are said to conflict whenever one reads a data item that the other intends to write or both transactions intend to write the same data item.) When transactions conflict, the possibility of an inconsistent result exists. In the preceding example, it would be possible to sell the same seat more than once or to update the number of seats sold improperly. One common solution to this problem is to incorporate a locking mechanism to prevent the simultaneous access by two different transactions from causing erroneous results.

Two types of locks, *exclusive locks* and *shared locks* are commonly used (Date 1977). An exclusive lock guarantees the holder that it is the only one with access to the locked entity. A shared lock, on the other hand, allows multiple holders to access the locked item, but guarantees that no transaction will change the locked entity while it is locked. We note that the use of locks introduces the possibility of deadlock (Coffman and Denning 1973), but since this is a global system problem we do not consider it further here.

One important decision concerning the use of locks is the locking *granularity*, that is, the size of the entity to be locked. If entire files are locked this has the effect of forcing transactions to run serially, whereas with conventional locking schemes, if smaller units such as records are locked, the resulting storage of lock tables and computational overhead to search them may become excessive. Wiederhold (1977) discusses these issues and others related to locking granularity. He indicates that the most common unit for locking is the block.

Eswaran et al. (1976) proposed a locking scheme based on simple predicates called *predicate locks*. This scheme allows for a variable locking granularity from file to field. Simply stated, a predicate lock locks the subset of a file satisfying some specified predicate. In the remainder of this section we discuss an implementation of predicate locks for IDAM files, called *combination locks*.

A predicate lock, L, is a pair $L = (P, U)$ where P is some predicate admissible under the encoding method and U is the set of all attribute-value pairs covered by the predicate together with the intended usage. More formally,

$$U = \{(a,v,u)|(a,v) \text{ is atomic in } P \text{ and } u \in \{s, x\}\}.$$

Here u denotes the requested usage for (a,v) where s denotes a shared lock and x denotes an exclusive lock. It will be convenient to partition U into two sets as determined by the intended usage of the members: U_s, the set of elements in U for which shared locks are being requested; and U_x, the set of elements in U for which exclusive locks are being requested. That is,

$$U_s = \{(a, v, u \in U \,|\, u = s\},$$

and

$$U_x = \{(a, v, u) \in U \,|\, u = x\}.$$

Let Λ represent the current state of the system, that is,

$$\Lambda = \{(a, v, u)|(a, v) \text{ is locked for usage } u \text{ by some } L\}.$$

Note here that the association between the predicates and the attribute-value pairs is lost. This results from the assumption that all attribute-value pairs specified by the predicates are explicitly represented in Λ.

Let $L(F)$ denote the subset of the file F to be locked by a particular predicate lock L, that is

$$L(F) = \{R \in F|P(R)\}.$$

Similarly, let $\Lambda(F)$ denote that portion of the file F locked by all the predicate locks currently outstanding in the system, or

$$\Lambda(F) = \{R \in F \,|\, P(R) \text{ for some } L = (P,U)\}.$$

To determine whether a predicate lock can be granted, it is necessary to consider the lock request with respect to all currently outstanding locks. This must be done to ascertain whether any conflict exists that would prevent the lock request from being granted. Recall that a conflict exists whenever two processes attempt to write the same entity or when one process attempt to write an entity that some other process is reading. If $L(F) \cap \Lambda(F) = \varnothing$, then no conflict can possibly exist since the lock request specifies unlocked attributes. However, when $L(F) \cap \Lambda(F) \neq \varnothing$, a potential conflict exists since this implies that

$$U \cap \Lambda \neq \varnothing. \tag{3.1}$$

Condition (3.1) is sufficient to detect a potential conflict. What is needed, however, is a simple test to detect actual conflicts. Let Λ_x denote the subset of Λ for which exclusive locks have been granted, that is,

$$\Lambda_x = \{(a, v, u) \in \Lambda \,|\, u = x\}.$$

Observation. A request for a predicate lock L contains a conflict if and only if

$$\left[U_x \cap \Lambda \neq \varnothing \right] \text{ OR } \left[U_s \cap \Lambda_x \neq \varnothing \right]. \tag{3.2}$$

This condition says that an actual conflict exists if either: (1) a requested exclusive lock conflicts with any outstanding lock; or (2) a requested shared lock conflicts with an existing exclusive lock. Condition (3.2) is necessary and sufficient to detect lock conflicts. For our purposes, however, an equivalent form of (3.2) will be more convenient. That is,

$$\left[U_x \cap \Lambda \neq \varnothing \right] \text{ OR } \left[U \cap \Lambda_x \neq \varnothing \right] \tag{3.3}$$

Here we have altered (3.2) to test for any requested lock conflicting with an existing exclusive lock. A particularly efficient method for testing condition (3.3) can be implemented to support combination locks.

Given a predicate lock $L = (P,U)$ and an encoding method E, we define a combination lock, L_c, to be the pair

$$L_c = \left(D(U), D(U_x) \right).$$

Recall that U is the set of all attributes specified by the predicate lock L, thus under the encoding E, $D(U)$ is a descriptor or bit string representation for the predicate. Similarly, since $U_x \subseteq U$ is the subset of U for which exclusive locks have been requested, $D(U_x)$ is the descriptor of U_x under E.

Two facts should be noted. First, combination locks are confined to those predicates which are admissible under the encoding method E. These predicates will typically be simple conjunctions, but as outlined in section 2.3, may be more expressive. Secondly, a combination lock L_c will in general lock a superset of the records requested by the equivalent predicate lock L. Thus, a combination lock may be coarser than the predicate lock depending ultimately on the encoding method E.

To implement combination locks we assume that the current system state is maintained as the pair $\left(D(\Lambda), D(\Lambda_x)\right)$ where $D(\Lambda)$ is the descriptor for the set, Λ, of all outstanding locks and $D(\Lambda_x)$ is the descriptor for the subset of Λ for which exclusive locks have been granted. Since the set representation for descriptors is a bit vector, the operations of intersection and union can be implemented directly with the boolean *AND* and *OR* respectively. Condition (3.3) can be implemented simply as

$$\left(D(U_x) \wedge D(\Lambda)\right) \vee \left(D(U) \wedge D(\Lambda_x)\right). \qquad (3.4)$$

If (3.4) is equal to **0,** no conflict exists and a lock request can be granted. Otherwise, the lock request may not be honored until the conflict is resolved.

Figure 3.4.   Algorithm to Screen Combination Lock Requests

```
function request( D(U ),D(U_x )) : request_type;
begin
      if ( D(U_x)∧ D(Λ))∨( D(U )∧ D(Λ_x )) = 0 then
          begin
                D(Λ) := D(Λ)∨ D(U );
                D(Λ_x ) := D(Λ_x )∨ D(U_x );
                save( D(U ));
                request := granted;
          end
      else
                request := denied;
end;
```

Using condition (3.4) to screen for lock conflicts, the algorithm *request* shown in figure 3.4 will implement a simple locking policy. The algorithm first checks to see if the request can be granted. If it can be granted, the system state is updated to reflect the new state. Otherwise, the lock is denied. Other courses of action are available when a conflict is detected. The request could be queued or some process preempted. The resolution of the lock request when a conflict occurs will depend on the locking policy adopted. Here we have chosen to deny the request since we are concerned with the locking mechanism not the policy.

The procedure call *save* ($D(U)$) needs some explanation. It is included to ensure that the system state is maintained properly when a lock is released. The operation of releasing a lock must be treated with some care. Since exclusive locks can only be held by one process it is sufficient when releasing them to remove them from Λ and Λ_x. Shared locks on the other hand can be held by multiple processes and therefore can only be removed from Λ when the last process releases them. This problem can be solved in several ways. One approach involves saving the parameter $D(U)$ from each lock request in a table, say *Saved_DU*. In this way the set Λ can be reconstructed after a lock is released. This is demonstrated by the algorithm *release* of figure 3.5. It is assumed that the procedures *save* and *remove* access the same table, *Saved_DU*. Note in figure 3.5 that the notation $A - B$ denotes the relative complement, that is, the complement of B in A. The corresponding bit vector operation is the exclusive-OR.

Figure 3.5. Algorithm to Release Combination Locks

$$\text{procedure } release(D(U), D(U_x));$$

$$\text{begin}$$

$$\quad remove(D(U));$$

$$\quad \Lambda := \mathbf{0};$$

$$\quad \text{for all } D(U) \epsilon \, Saved\_DU \text{ do}$$

$$\quad\quad D(\Lambda) := D(\Lambda) \vee D(U);$$

$$\quad D(\Lambda_x) := D(\Lambda_x) - D(U_x);$$

$$\text{end};$$

As an example of the use of combination locks note that a query Q can request shared access to an IDAM file with the lock request ($D(Q),\mathbf{0}$). If the query also wanted to guarantee the state of some unspecified values, a separate mask $D(U)$ would be necessary. As with predicate locks, combination locks can be used to specify a wide range of locking granularities from the entire file (**1,0**) or (**1,1**) for shared or exclusive access, respectively) to fields and values within fields.

As we observed earlier, a combination lock will, in general, lock a superset of the records intended by the corresponding predicate lock, or $L(F) \subseteq L_c(F)$. This means that the locking granularity will lie somewhere between predicate locks and conventional locking schemes depending primarily on the encoding method used.

With combination locks it is possible to allow index activity while preventing access into the data level of the IDAM file. For example, a search may be allowed to proceed until it attempts to access a data block exclusively locked by some other process. The search will then have to be suspended until the lock is released. At that point, before the search actually accesses the data block, the query descriptor should be rechecked against the block descriptor. This will in some cases prevent an unnecessary block access.

The combination lock could actually be enforced at the record (field) level. However, since this introduces the possibility of lost updates due to multiple copies of a block, it seems more reasonable to enforce the lock at the block level.

The implementation of combination locks outlined in this section is not a locking protocol. It does not address the important issues of deadlock avoidance or prevention, but does serve to illustrate the potential of IDAM files for concurrent applications. These issues while important are related to a locking policy not the locking mechanism, and are not considered here.

3.4   Storage Requirements

We can estimate the storage overhead due to the index as follows. Let *size* (x) denote the size in bits of the argument x. We assume that *size* (x) takes into consideration any alignment restrictions imposed by specific hardware. This eliminates unnecessary complexity due to differing byte and word sizes on different machines.

The size of an index is the sum of the file sizes each of which is the product of the number of blocks times the block size. Let B_i denote a block at level i. Then

$$size\ (index) \ = \ \sum_{i=1}^{h} \ size\ (F_i)$$

$$= \ \sum_{i=1}^{h} \ n_i\ size\ (B_i), \quad B_i \in F_i. \tag{3.5}$$

Throughout we will assume that N_i/b_i is an integer, that is, all blocks are assumed to be fully packed. This will not introduce any loss of generality. To see this, consider a data file $F = \{R_1, R_2, \ldots, R_N\}$ having b records per block such that $N/b < \lceil N/b \rceil$. If the last record, R_N is replicated $(b \lceil N/b \rceil - N)$ times, a new file F' results with $N'/b = \lceil N/b \rceil$. Clearly, F and F' will give rise to the same D-tree. Hence, F and F' will have the same performance characteristics. In addition, since secondary storage is ordinarily allocated in integral units, F and F' will have the same storage requirement. To extend this assumption about fully packed blocks to the index levels, we assume that partially packed blocks are padded with 0-descriptors.

Since the number of records at level i is equal to the number of blocks at level $i - 1$, we have

$$n_i = \frac{N_i}{b_i} = \frac{n_{i-1}}{b_i}.$$

From the initial condition $n_0 = N/b_0$, it is easy to see that this recurrence has the solution

$$n_i = \frac{N}{\prod\limits_{k=0}^{i} b_k}, \quad i = 0, 1, \ldots, h. \tag{3.6}$$

This cumbersome product has a simple interpretation. Let r_i denote the number of data records covered by a descriptor at level i. It is clear that r_i satisfies the recurrence

$$r_i = b_{i-1} r_{i-1}, \quad r_1 = b_0.$$

Therefore

$$r_i = \prod_{k=0}^{i-1} b_k, \quad i = 1, 2, \ldots, h.$$

Substituting back into (3.6) yields

$$n_i = \frac{N}{\prod\limits_{k=0}^{i} b_k} = \frac{N}{b_i r_i} = \frac{N}{r_{i+1}}, \quad i = 0, 1, \ldots, h. \tag{3.7}$$

Thus, from equation (3.5) the size of the index is given by

$$size\ (index) = N \sum_{i=1}^{h} \frac{1}{r_{i+1}} \, size\ (B_i). \tag{3.8}$$

The size of an index block can be determined by examining figure 3.1. Each index block B_i requires at least enough storage for b_i descriptors and $b_i + 2$ pointers. Hence,

$$size\ (B_i) = wb_i + (b_i + 2)\ size\ (pointer),$$

where the first term follows from the fact that all descriptors have width w. Combining with equation (3.8) gives the following expression for index size

$$size \ (index) = N \sum_{i=1}^{h} \frac{1}{r_{i+1}} \left[wb_i + (b_i + 2) size \ (pointer) \right]. \qquad (3.9)$$

To simplify further, let $size \ (pointer) = \alpha w \ (0 \leqslant \alpha < 1)$. This is not an unreasonable assumption; in fact we would expect a pointer to be significantly smaller than a descriptor in general. Substituting into equation (3.9) yields

$$size \ (index) = N \sum_{i=1}^{h} \frac{1}{r_{i+1}} \left[wb_i + (b_i + 2)\alpha w \right]$$

$$= wN \sum_{i=1}^{h} \frac{1}{b_i r_i} \left[(1 + \alpha)b_i + 2\alpha \right]$$

$$= (1 + \alpha)wN \sum_{i=1}^{h} \frac{1}{r_i} + 2\alpha wN \sum_{i=1}^{h} \frac{1}{b_i r_i} . \qquad (3.10)$$

Although equation (3.10) can be used to calculate the size of an index, its interpretation is made simpler by recalling that (cf. equation 3.7)

$$n_i = \frac{N}{b_i r_i} .$$

Therefore,

$$N_i = b_i n_i = \frac{N}{r_i} ,$$

so that (3.10) can be rewritten to explicitly show the contribution of each of its components that is,

$$size \ (index) = (1 + \alpha)w \sum_{i=1}^{h} N_i + 2\alpha w \sum_{i=1}^{h} n_i$$

$$= w \sum_{i=1}^{h} N_i + \alpha w \sum_{i=1}^{h} N_i + 2\alpha w \sum_{i=1}^{h} n_i .$$

Equation (3.10) can be simplified further for the special case where $b_i = b$, $i > 0$ (that is, when all the index blocking factors are the same, but not necessarily the same as b_0). When this is the case, equation (3.10) can be simplified by noting that

$$\sum_{i=1}^{h} \frac{1}{r_i} = \frac{1}{r_1} + \sum_{i=2}^{h} \frac{1}{r_i} = \frac{1}{b_0} + \sum_{i=2}^{h} \frac{1}{b^i} ,$$

where

$$\sum_{i=2}^{h} \frac{1}{b^i}$$

is a geometric series. The closed form for this expression is

$$\sum_{i=2}^{h} \frac{1}{b^i} = \begin{cases} \dfrac{b^{h-1} - 1}{b^h(b - 1)}, & b > 1 \\ h - 1, & b = 1. \end{cases}$$

The situation where $b_i = b$, $i > 0$ is not unrealistic and has the advantage of simplifying the management of the index files. We will not pursue this any further except to note that under this assumption, it can be shown that

$$size\ (index) < (1 + 3\alpha)wN \left[\frac{1}{b_0} + \frac{1}{b(b - 1)} \right].$$

The minimal index size will be achieved when $\alpha = 0$, that is, when no pointers are used. This is in fact possible as the following discussion will demonstrate.

Recall that each level of an IDAM file is required to be logically contiguous. If instead we make each level physically contiguous, a particularly compact representation is possible. In this case we are able to represent all pointers implicitly rather than explicitly and thus, reduce the overall storage requirement.

Clearly, we no longer need the *next* pointer as a direct result of the physical continuity. We can eliminate the *son* pointers as follows. Assume that blocks and entries are numbered from one. Suppose we want to find the block in level $i - 1$ described by the dth descriptor in some block B_{i,β_i} *at level i*. Here β_i $(1 \leqslant \beta_i \leqslant n_i)$ is the block number and d $(1 \leqslant d \leqslant b_i)$ is the number of the particular descriptor within block β_i. The block number β_{i-1} of the block in question is given by

$$\beta_{i-1} = (\beta_i - 1)n_i + d.$$

Thus, knowing the pair (β_i, d) implicitly determines the *son* block and no pointer is necessary.

Similarly, we can eliminate the *parent* pointers. In this case, we want to find the pair (β_{i+1}, d) corresponding to the parent descriptor of some block B_{i,β_i}. Since the block number β_i corresponds to the β_i-th entry in the index level $i + 1$, we have

$$\beta_{i+1} = \left\lfloor \frac{\beta_i - 1}{b_{i+1}} \right\rfloor + 1$$

$$d = \beta_i - (\beta_{i+1} - 1)b_{i+1}.$$

Hence, we are able to eliminate all the explicit pointers from the IDAM file representation. It follows from equation (3.10) that the index size will be

$$size \ (index) = wN \sum_{i=1}^{h} \frac{1}{r_i} = w \sum_{i=1}^{h} N_i \ , \tag{3.11}$$

which as expected is just the width of a descriptor times the number of descriptors in all the index levels. The premium exacted for this reduction in storage overhead is a modest increase in computational overhead.

Equation (3.11) can be considered a lower bound on the size of an index. Let S_{min} denote this quantity. To more fully assess the storage penalty involved when pointers are used, rewrite equation (3.10) in terms of S_{min}. That is,

$$size \ (index) = (1 + \alpha)S_{min} + 2\alpha wN \sum_{i=1}^{h} \frac{1}{b_i r_i}$$

$$\leqslant (1 + \alpha)S_{min} + 2\alpha wN \sum_{i=1}^{h} \frac{1}{r_i} \ ,$$

with equality holding when $b_i = 1$ for all i. This implies that

$$(1 + \alpha)S_{min} < size \ (index) \leqslant (1 + 3\alpha)S_{min}.$$

Therefore, a linked representation of an index can be expected to be between α and 3α percent larger than the minimal representation of the index. For example, since a pointer will normally be 16 or 32 bits, the increase in the size of the index will be 16–48 and 32–96 percent, respectively, given a width $w = 100$ descriptor.

4

Randomly Organized IDAM Files

In this chapter we consider the behavior of D-trees indexing randomly organized data files. By randomly organized data file we mean only that a file F has been constructed from records entered in some arbitrary and unspecified order. In particular, it is not assumed that some "randomizing" technique has been applied to the data records.

The importance of understanding the behavior of D-trees indexing files organized in this manner stems from the following considerations:

1. This organization results in the simplest of all D-tree structures and thus, if performance is adequate, may be quite suitable for many applications; and
2. The performance of the resulting D-tree structures represents a baseline against which the performance of more sophisticated structures can be compared.

We begin the analysis by reviewing the work of Pfaltz et al. on the expected number of accesses per query.

4.1 Expected Number of Accesses per Query

Pfaltz, Berman and Cagley (1980) have analyzed the retrieval algorithm DFS of figure 3.3 to determine the expected number of secondary storage accesses under certain assumptions. Although they were concerned specifically with a weight-1 disjoint encoding method, in which only one bit is set per field, their results can be shown to have wider application. We will review their analysis here and identify the assumptions under which it is applicable.

In the following discussion we assume that a query Q with descriptor $D(Q)$ is to be answered by a retrieval system using an IDAM file (i.e., a D-tree of height h over the data file) as the retrieval mechanism. The search is assumed to start at the highest index level h.

Let $\rho_i(Q)$ denote the probability that $D(Q)$ will match a descriptor $D(i)$ at level i in a tree, or

$$\rho_i(Q) = Pr(D(Q) \wedge D(i) = D(Q), D(i) \in F_i).$$

Let $\rho_j(i)$ denote the probability that field j of $D(Q)$ matches field j of any descriptor at level i, or

$$\rho_j(i) = Pr(D_j(Q) \wedge D_j(i) = D_j(Q), D_i(i) \in F_i),$$

where $D_j(i)$ denotes the jth field of the descriptor $D(i) \in F_i$. We will assume throughout that the probability of matching a field in a descriptor is independent of the probability of matching any other field. Therefore, $\rho_i(Q) = \Pi_{j \in Q} \rho_j(i)$. Again, the notation $j \in Q$ denotes the q fields specified in the query Q.

In any partial match retrieval, all the descriptors at the highest level, h, must be examined. We therefore begin the analysis by considering the expected number of blocks accessed at level $h - 1$. Since each descriptor in level h corresponds to a block in level $h - 1$, we have only to determine the expected number of descriptors matched in level h. Assuming that we are equally likely to match any descriptor in level h, the expected number of matches is given by

$$N_h \rho_h(Q), \tag{4.1}$$

where by the independence assumption

$$\rho_h(Q) = \prod_{j \in Q} \rho_j(h), \tag{4.2}$$

and denotes the probability that $D(Q)$ will match any descriptor in level h. Let $\bar{a}_i(Q)$ denote the expected number of blocks (nodes) accessed at level i to satisfy the query Q. Combining (4.1) with equation (4.2), we have for the expected number of accesses in level $h - 1$,

$$\bar{a}_{h-1}(Q) = N_h \prod_{j \in Q} \rho_j(h). \tag{4.3}$$

To proceed further we must consider the effects of the encoding method. Pfaltz et al. performed this analysis with respect to a weight-1 disjoint encoding method. As we will see, their result is robust enough to accommodate many weight-k encoding methods. If we assume that each bit in a field is equally likely to be set, it follows that

$$\rho_j(h) = \frac{\bar{s}_j(h)}{w_j},$$

where $\bar{s}_j(h)$ denotes the average number of bits set in field j and the average is taken over all the descriptors in level h. Under this assumption, equation (4.3) can be rewritten as

$$\bar{a}_{h-1}(Q) = N_h \prod_{j \in Q} \frac{\bar{s}_j(h)}{w_j}, \tag{4.4}$$

We now consider the number of accesses at level $h - 2$ ($h \geqslant 2$). The number of blocks accessed at level $h - 2$ is precisely the number of descriptor matches occurring among the blocks of descriptors accessed at level $h - 1$. We must examine all $b_{h-1}\bar{a}_{h-1}$ descriptors accessed and fetch a block at level $h - 2$ whenever a match occurs. To determine the expected number of matches given that a block has been accessed, notice that the effective width of a field j has been reduced from w_j to $\bar{s}_j(h)$ by virtue of the access. Thus, the probability that $D(Q)$ will match some descriptor $D \in B_{h-1}$ is

$$\frac{\bar{s}_j\,(h - 1)}{\bar{s}_j(h)} \ .$$

Therefore the expected number of accesses at level $h - 2$ is given by

$$\bar{a}_{h-2}(Q) = b_{h-1}\bar{a}_{h-1}(Q) \prod_{j \in Q} \left[\frac{\bar{s}_j(h - 1)}{\bar{s}_j(h)} \right].$$

Substituting equation (4.4) into this expression yields

$$\bar{a}_{h-2}(Q) = b_{h-1} \left[N_h \prod_{j \in Q} \frac{\bar{s}_j(h)}{w_j} \right] \prod_{j \in Q} \left[\frac{\bar{s}_j(h - 1)}{\bar{s}_j(h)} \right]$$

$$= b_{h-1} N_h \prod_{j \in Q} \frac{\bar{s}_j(h - 1)}{w_j} \ .$$

But since the number of records in level h equals the number of blocks in level $h - 1$, it follows that $b_{h-1}N_h = b_{h-1}n_{h-1} - N_{h-1}$. Hence,

$$\bar{a}_{h-2}(Q) = N_{h-1} \prod_{j \in Q} \frac{\bar{s}_j(h - 1)}{w_j} \ ,$$

which just says that the expected number of accesses at level $h - 2$ is equal to the expected number of matches at level $h - 1$ if level $h - 1$ were scanned sequentially. In an entirely analogous manner it can be shown that when searching an index at level i the expected number of accesses to the file at level $i - 1$ is given by

$$\bar{a}_{i-1}(Q) = N_i \prod_{j \in Q} \frac{\bar{s}_j(i)}{w_j} \ . \tag{4.5}$$

The total expected number of accesses, $\bar{a}(Q)$, is the sum of the expected accesses at each level. Therefore

$$\bar{a}(Q) = \sum_{i=0}^{h} \bar{a}_i(Q) = \bar{a}_h(Q) + \sum_{i=1}^{h} \bar{a}_{i-1}(Q).$$

Combining with equation (4.5) yields

$$\bar{a}(Q) = \bar{a}_h(Q) + \sum_{i=1}^{h} N_i \prod_{j \in Q} \frac{\bar{s}_j(i)}{w_j} . \qquad (4.6)$$

This is the main result of the paper by Pfaltz, Berman and Cagley, and shows very clearly the dependence of retrieval performance on the average number of bits set in each field.

The quantity $\bar{a}_h(Q)$ represents the expected number of accesses at the highest index level. If the highest level is reread for every query, then $\bar{a}_h(Q) = n_h$, since all the blocks must be fetched. Alternatively, if the highest level is resident in main memory, then $\bar{a}_h(Q) \rightarrow 0$, since it is amortized over all the queries presented to the system.

Equation (4.6) will serve as the basis of our subsequent analysis of the performance of D-trees. The two specific assumptions used to derive it are:

1. The probability of matching any field in a descriptor is independent of all other fields.
2. Each bit in a descriptor at level i is equally likely to be set.

Inspection of (4.6) shows that $\bar{a}(Q)$ can be calculated if $\bar{s}_j(i)$ is known. The thrust of our analysis is to find expressions for this quantity given various file organizations. The notation $\bar{s}_j(i)$ is an abbreviation for the expected number of bits set in field j of a descriptor at level i and does not fully capture the functional dependence on the various system parameters. It should be clear that $\bar{s}_j(i)$ depends on the field width, the number of records covered by a descriptor, and potentially other factors as well.

It should be noted that $\bar{a}(Q)$ does not necessarily represent the fewest accesses possible to satisfy a query when using a D-tree. As an extreme example, if level h consisted of fully saturated descriptors, $D = 1$ for all $D \in F_h$, then all the blocks at level $h - 1$ would have to be read. In this case, it would be possible to reduce the expected number of accesses by starting the search at level $h - 1$. Consider the null query. Since its descriptor is $D(Q) = 0$ it will match any descriptor in the D-tree. Hence, a naive search routine will read every block in every level in order to satisfy this query. Clearly, only the data level should be read. The following discussion introduces a rule for deciding at which level in the tree a search should be started to minimize $\sum_i \bar{a}_i(Q)$.

Suppose we have a D-tree of height h. There are N_i descriptors in each level i of the tree. These descriptors are grouped into

$$n_i = \frac{N_i}{b_i}$$

blocks. We have already observed that algorithm *DFS* of figure 3.3 will work correctly irrespective of which level is chosen as the "root" of the tree. We would like to start the search at the level which results in the most efficient retrieval. The *optimal access strategy* specifies for each query the starting level in the tree which minimizes the expected number of block accesses needed to satisfy the query.

Let Q be a query on q attributes. The probability that $D(Q)$ will match one of the N_i descriptors at level i is, by the field independence assumption, the product of the q field match probabilities $\rho_j(i)$ such that $j \in Q$. Recall that this probability is denoted by $\rho_i(Q)$, where

$$\rho_i(Q) = \prod_{j \in Q} \rho_j(i) .$$

Since the retrieval algorithm must search all the descriptors in the level of the tree chosen as the root for the search, we have if that level is k, $\bar{a}_k(Q) = n_k$. The following result specifies $\bar{a}_i(Q)$ for the remaining levels of the tree.

Lemma 4.1: The expected number of blocks (nodes) accessed at level i in a D-tree to satisfy a query Q is

$$\bar{a}_i(Q) = N_{i+1}\rho_{i+1}(Q), \ 0 \leqslant i < k,$$

where k denotes the level at which the search is started. Moreover, this is true irrespective of where the search is started as long as $k \geqslant 1$.

Proof: Let $\bar{A}_i(Q)$ denote the expected number of descriptors that Q will match from among the N_i descriptors at level i. Note that the expected number of blocks accessed at level i is equal to the expected number of descriptors matched in level $i + 1$, or

$$\bar{a}_i(Q) = \bar{A}_{i+1}(Q).$$

The probability that $D(Q)$ will match any descriptor in level $i + 1$ is $\rho_{i+1}(Q)$. Let X be the discrete random variable denoting the number of matches occurring. Since Q is equally likely to match any descriptor at level i, X is binomially distributed with probability of success $\rho_{i+1}(Q)$. Thus, the expected number of matches is

$$\bar{A}_{i+1}(Q) = E\left[X \mid Q \right] = N_{i+1}\rho_{i+1}(Q)$$

which is the desired result. $\square$

The optimal access strategy seeks to minimize $\Sigma\ \bar{a}_i(Q)$. Lemma 4.1 can be used to derive a computationally easy rule for incorporating this strategy into the search process.

Theorem 4.2: The optimal access strategy when searching a *D*-tree is to start the search at the highest level *i* in the tree such that

$$\rho_i(Q) < 1 - \frac{1}{b_i}, \quad 0 < i \leqslant h,$$

where b_i is the number of descriptors in a block at level *i*. If no level *i*, $0 < i \leqslant h$, satisfies this condition, the index should not be used; that is, the data file should be read directly.

Proof: Since the optimal access strategy seeks to minimize $\Sigma\ \bar{a}_i(Q)$, we conclude that the search should be started at the highest level such that

$$n_i + \bar{a}_{i-1}(Q) < n_{i-1}.$$

That is, to start at level *i* the number of blocks accessed at level *i* plus the expected number of accesses at the next level should be less than accessing all the blocks at the next level. If this were not true then $\Sigma\ \bar{a}_i(Q)$ could be reduced by starting the search at level $i - 1$.

Since $n_i = N_i/b_i$ and $N_i = n_{i-1}$, the inequality can be written as

$$\frac{N_i}{b_i} + \bar{a}_{i-1}(Q) < N_i.$$

Applying lemma 4.1 yields

$$\frac{N_i}{b_i} + N_i\rho_i(Q) < N_i,$$

from which the result now follows immediately. □

The optimal access strategy can be implemented by maintaining an $h \times f$ matrix of the field match probabilities, $\rho_j(i)$, from which $\rho_i(Q)$ is easily computed.

An obvious corollary is immediate from theorem 4.2.

Corollary 4.2.1: The null query should read only the data level.

Proof: Since the null query specifies no attributes, $D(Q) = 0$ and will match every descriptor. Hence, $\rho_i(Q) = 1$ and theorem 4.2 will not be satisfied for any level $i > 0$. □

Theorem 4.2 also supports the intuitive feeling that no index level should have a blocking factor equal to one.

Corollary 4.2.2: It never pays to create a D-tree with any level having one entry per block ($b_i = 1$).

Proof: By theorem 4.2, it is apparent that no search will ever start at any level i with $b_i = 1$. Now consider an interior level i in the tree with $b_i = 1$ and assume that by theorem 4.2 some level $k > i$ is selected as the search starting point. Since $b_i = 1$, we have two identical levels in the tree and hence, $\rho_{i+1}(Q) = \rho_i(Q)$. Thus, all the accesses at level i are superfluous and can be eliminated with no reduction in retrieval performance. $\square$

In the remainder of this book we will investigate specific organizations of the data and index files with respect to retrieval performance. The evaluation of retrieval performance will consider secondary storage accesses as the cost criterion of interest. Specifically, we will analyze competing methods to determine the expected number of secondary storage accesses necessary to satisfy a query.

4.2 Expected Bit Densities

We have seen that the expected number of accesses per query in a D-tree depends on the average bit density of the descriptors at each level in the tree. In this section we will derive an expression for the quantity $\bar{s}_j(t)$ of equation (4.6) for the case of randomly organized files.

Suppose we have a random sample of $r \geqslant 1$ weight-1 binary strings each of width w, say $\Sigma_1, \Sigma_2, \ldots, \Sigma_r$. Let

$$\vee \Sigma_i = \bigvee_{i=1}^{r} \Sigma_i$$

denote the logical sum or inclusive-OR of the Σ_i. Let X be the discrete random variable given by $X = weight\,(\vee \Sigma_i)$. The value of X is the number of bits set in the width w code formed from the logical sum of the Σ_i. Let $s(t)$ denote the probability mass function (pmf) of X. That is,

$$s(t) = Pr(X = t) = Pr(weight\,(\vee \Sigma_i) = t), \quad 0 \leqslant t \leqslant w.$$

What we want to find is an expression for $s(t)$.

Before proceeding, we need to develop some preliminary notation. Let us denote the bit string Σ_i by $(\sigma_1, \sigma_2, \ldots, \sigma_w)$ where $\sigma_k \in \{0, 1\}$. Since each Σ_i is weight-1, exactly one bit is set in the bit string. Let $bit\,(\Sigma_i)$ denote that bit. Thus, $bit\,(\Sigma_i) = k$ if and only if $\sigma_k = 1$. We can now prove the following result.

Theorem 4.3: X has pmf given by

$$s(t) = \frac{C_t^w S_t^r t!}{w^r},$$

where C_k^n denotes the number of combinations of n objects taken k at a time; and S_k^n is a Stirling number of the second kind denoting the number of ways to partition a set of n objects into exactly k nonempty subsets.

Proof: Let $\mathbf{S}(r)$ denote the set of all possible r-tuples $(\Sigma_1, \Sigma_2, \ldots, \Sigma_r)$,

$$\mathbf{S}(r) = \{(\Sigma_1, \Sigma_2, \ldots, \Sigma_r) \mid weight\ (\Sigma_i) = 1\}.$$

Clearly, $|\mathbf{S}(r)| = w^r$. To count the number of ways to set a prespecified t bits in $\vee \Sigma_i$, note that this is equivalent to counting the number of ways to have all bits set in $\vee \Sigma_i'$ of width t since the remaining $w - t$ bits in $\vee \Sigma_i$ must all be zero. Now consider the set

$$\mathbf{S}_t(r) = \{(\Sigma_1, \Sigma_2, \ldots, \Sigma_r) \in \mathbf{S}(r) \mid bit(\Sigma_i) \leqslant t\}.$$

This is the subset of $\mathbf{S}(r)$ containing r-tuples with components of the form

$$(\sigma_1, \sigma_2, \ldots, \sigma_t, \sigma_{t+1}, \ldots, \sigma_{w-1}, \sigma_w),$$

where the 1-bit occurs somewhere in the first t positions.

Notice that we could create a similar set from any other t bit positions. In fact, there are C_t^w such sets and they partition $\mathbf{S}(r)$. It is also clear that each set will have the same cardinality and the same number of elements with $weight(\vee \Sigma_i) = t$. Therefore it suffices to count the number of r-tuples in $\mathbf{S}_t(r)$ with $weight(\vee \Sigma_i) = t$. Thus, the pmf will have the form

$$s(t) = \frac{1}{w^r}\ C_t^w\ [\text{number of elements in } \mathbf{S}_t(r) \text{ with } weight(\vee \Sigma_i) = t]. \quad (4.7)$$

Let $a_i \equiv i^{\text{th}}$ bit has value zero, $1 \leqslant i \leqslant t$ and let $a'_i \equiv i^{\text{th}}$ bit has value one. In the notation of Liu (1968), we let N be the cardinality of the set $\mathbf{S}_t(r)$ and we let $N(x_{i_1}, x_{i_2}, \ldots, x_{i_j})$, where x is replaced by a or a', denote the cardinality of the subset of $\mathbf{S}_t(r)$ having the j specified properties. Thus, we want to find $N(a'_1, a'_2, \ldots, a'_t)$, which is the number of ways all t bits can be set. By the principle of inclusion and exclusion

$$N(a'_1, a'_2, \ldots, a'_t) = N - \sum_i N(a_i) + \sum_{i \neq j} N(a_i, a_j) - \ldots$$

$$+ (-1)^t N(a_1, a_2, \ldots, a_t) \quad (4.8)$$

The jth sum in this expression will have C_j^t terms of equal value (by symmetry). Letting N_j denote that value in the jth sum, we can rewrite (4.8) as

$$N(a'_1, a'_2, \ldots, a'_t) = C_0^t N_0 - C_1^t N_1 + C_2^t N_2 - \ldots + (-1)^t C_t^t N_t$$

$$= \sum_{j=0}^{t} (-1)^j C_j^t N_j . \tag{4.9}$$

To determine N_j, note that in order to be included in a count, each string in an r-tuple must have zeros in j places and ones or zeros in the remaining $t - j$ places. Since each string has exactly one bit set, there are $t - j$ positions that bit may occupy. Thus, N_j can be written as $N_j = (t - j)^r$. Substituting this value for N_j in (4.9) yields

$$N(a'_1, a'_2, \ldots, a'_t) = \sum_{j=0}^{t} (-1)^j C_j^t (t - j)^r$$

$$= S_t^r t! , \tag{4.10}$$

where S_t^r is a Stirling number of the second kind (Liu 1968, p. 38) Thus, $s(t)$ can now be obtained by substituting (4.10) into (4.7) and is given by

$$s(t) = \frac{C_t^w S_t^r t!}{w^r} . \tag{4.11}$$

Clearly, $s(t) \geqslant 0$, $1 \leqslant t \leqslant w$. Moreover, since $S_0^r = 0$ and $C_t^w = 0$ ($t > w$), it follows that $s(0) = 0$ and $s(t) = 0$ ($t > w$). We now have only to show that

$$\sum_t s(t) = 1.$$

But, this follows immediately from the identity

$$x^n = \sum_k S_k^n C_k^x k!$$

(Knuth 1973, vol. 1). Thus, (4.11) is a proper probability mass function. $\square$

We will make use of the moment generating function given in the next theorem to calculate the mean and variance of the random variable X of theorem 4.3.

Theorem 4.4: Let X be the discrete random variable with pmf given by

$$s(t) = \frac{C_t^w S_t^r t!}{w^r} .$$

X has the moment generating function given by

$$M(t) = \frac{e^{wt}}{w^r} \sum_{k=0}^{w} C_k^w (w - k)^r \left[\frac{1}{e^t} - 1 \right]^k .$$

Proof: Let

$$P(z) = \sum_{t=0}^{w} s(t) z^t$$

be the probability generating function (Coffman and Denning 1973) for $s(t)$. Our approach will be to find $P(z)$ and then use the identity $M(t) = P(e^t)$ (Larson 1969) to find the moment generating function, $M(t)$, for $s(t)$. First we rewrite $s(t)$ as

$$
\begin{aligned}
s(t) &= \frac{1}{w^r} \, C_t^w \sum_{j=0}^{t} (-1)^j C_j^t (t-j)^r \\
&= \frac{1}{w^r} \, C_t^w \sum_{j=0}^{t} (-1)^j C_{t-j}^t (t-j)^r \\
&= \frac{1}{w^r} \, C_t^w \sum_{k=0}^{t} (-1)^{t-k} C_k^t k^r ,
\end{aligned}
$$

where we have let $k = t - j$. From the definition of $P(z)$ we have

$$
\begin{aligned}
P(z) &= \sum_{t=0}^{w} \left[\frac{1}{w^r} \, C_t^w \sum_{k=0}^{t} (-1)^{t-k} C_k^t k^r \right] z^t \\
&= \frac{1}{w^r} \sum_{t=0}^{w} \sum_{k=0}^{t} (-1)^{t-k} C_t^w C_k^t k^r z^t \\
&= \frac{1}{w^r} \sum_{k=0}^{w} k^r \sum_{t=0}^{w} (-1)^{t-k} C_t^w C_k^t z^t .
\end{aligned}
\tag{4.12}
$$

Note that $C_t^w C_k^t = C_k^w C_{t-k}^{w-k}$ since

$$
\begin{aligned}
C_t^w C_k^t &= \frac{w!}{t!(w-t)!} \, \frac{t!}{k!(t-k)!} \\
&= \frac{w!}{k!(w-k)!} \, \frac{(w-k)!}{(w-t)!(t-k)!} = C_k^w C_{t-k}^{w-k}.
\end{aligned}
$$

Substituting into equation (4.12) yields

$$
\begin{aligned}
P(z) &= \frac{1}{w^r} \sum_{k=0}^{w} k^r C_k^w \sum_{t=0}^{w} (-1)^{t-k} C_{t-k}^{w-k} z^t \\
&= \frac{1}{w^r} \sum_{k=0}^{w} k^r C_k^w z^k \sum_{t=0}^{w} C_{t-k}^{w-k} (-z)^{t-k} \\
&= \frac{1}{w^r} \sum_{k=0}^{w} k^r C_k^w z^k \sum_{j=0}^{w-k} C_j^{w-k} (-z)^j ,
\end{aligned}
$$

where we have let $j = t - k$. Now applying the binomial theorem to the second sum yields

$$P(z) = \frac{1}{w^r} \sum_{k=0}^{w} k^r C_k^w z^k (1 - z)^{w-k}$$

$$= \frac{1}{w^r} \sum_{k=0}^{w} k^r C_{w-k}^w z^k (1 - z)^{w-k} .$$

Let $j = w - k$; then

$$P(z) = \frac{1}{w^r} \sum_{j=0}^{w} (w - j)^r C_j^w z^{w-j} (1 - z)^j$$

$$= \frac{z^w}{w^r} \sum_{j=0}^{w} C_j^w (w - j)^r \left(\frac{1}{z} - 1 \right)^j .$$

Thus, the moment generating function for $s(t)$ is given by

$$M(t) = P(e^t) = \frac{e^{wt}}{w^r} \sum_{k=0}^{w} C_k^w (w - k)^r \left(\frac{1}{e^t} - 1 \right)^k . \quad \Box$$

The next result yields the desired expression for the quanity $\bar{s}_j(i)$ of equation (4.6).

Corollary 4.4.1: Let X be the discrete random variable with pmf given by

$$s(t) = \frac{C_t^w S_t^r t!}{w^r} .$$

X has mean and variance given by

(a) $\mu(w,r) = w \left[1 - \left(1 - \frac{1}{w} \right)^r \right] .$

(b) $\sigma^2(w,r) = w \left(\frac{w-1}{w} \right)^r + w(w-1) \left(\frac{w-2}{w} \right)^r - w^2 \left(\frac{w-1}{w} \right)^{2r}$

$$= \left[w - \mu(w,r) \right] \left[\mu(w,r) - \mu(w-1,r) \right] .$$

The proof of this corollary is a straightforward but lengthy derivation using the moment generating function of theorem 4.4. The details of the proof are given in Appendix A.

The quantity in brackets in $\mu(w,r)$ of corollary 4.4.1(a) is just the probability that any bit will be set in $\vee \Sigma_i$. To see this consider an arbitrary bit position, say

σ_k, in $\vee \Sigma_i$. This bit will be set if *bit* $(\Sigma_i) = k$ for any of the r bit strings in $\vee \Sigma_i$. Alternatively, bit σ_k will not be set if all the Σ_i have $\sigma_k = 0$. Since

$$Pr(\sigma_k = 1) = \frac{1}{w},$$

it follows that

$$\left(1 - \frac{1}{w}\right)^r$$

is the probability that all the Σ_i will have $\sigma_k = 0$. Therefore,

$$1 - \left(1 - \frac{1}{w}\right)^r$$

is the probability that $\sigma_k = 1$ in $\vee \Sigma_i$.

The expected number of bits set in field j of a descriptor at level i in a randomly organized D-tree is, from corollary 4.4.1(a),

$$\bar{s}_j(i) = \mu(w_j, r_i),$$

where w_j is the field width and r_i is the number of data records covered by the descriptor. The next result shows how $\bar{s}_j(i)$ is affected by changes in the parameters w_j and r_i. This will be discussed more fully in the next section.

Corollary 4.4.2: The asymptotic behavior of the expressions given in corollary 4.4.1 for the mean and variance of the discrete random variable X can be characterized as follows.

(a) $\lim\limits_{r \to \infty} \mu(w, r) = w$ (d) $\lim\limits_{r \to \infty} \sigma^2(w, r) = 0$

(b) $\lim\limits_{w \to \infty} \mu(w, r) = r$ (e) $\lim\limits_{w \to \infty} \sigma^2(w, r) = 0$

(c) $\mu(w, 1) = \mu(1, r) = 1$ (f) $\sigma^2(w, 1) = \sigma^2(1, r) = 0$

The proof of this corollary involves routine but lengthy calculations and is also given in Appendix A.

Corollaries 4.4.1 and 4.4.2 provide a concise summary of the behavior of randomly organized files and accord well with intuition. The expected bit density is a monotone increasing function of w and r. As r grows without bound we expect every bit to ultimately be represented in a descriptor, whereas when w is allowed to grow while r is fixed, we expect precisely r bits to be set. If we have a single record per block (or as $w \to 1$), only one bit can be set. Corollary 4.4.2(d-f) shows that at these extreme values of r and w, the bit density approaches a constant.

An alternative, and somewhat more intuitive, derivation of the expected bit density for a single width w field is now presented. Suppose we have a block of r records. Let $X(r)$ denote the number of bits set in a descriptor for this block. Suppose we add a new descriptor to the block. It will match one of the existing bits with probability (w.p.) $X(r)/w$; it will be different w.p. $1 - X(r)/w$. Thus,

$$
X(r) = \begin{cases} X(r - 1) & \text{w.p. } X(r - 1)/w \\ X(r - 1) + 1 & \text{w.p. } 1 - X(r - 1)/w \end{cases}
$$

which gives rise to the following recurrence relation:

$$
E[X(r) \mid X(r - 1)] = 1 + \left(1 - \frac{1}{w} \right) X(r - 1). \qquad (4.13)
$$

Taking the expectation of both sides of equation (4.13) and letting $\bar{s}(r)$ denote $E[X(r)]$ yields the recurrence

$$
\bar{s}(r) = 1 + \left(1 + \frac{1}{w} \right) \bar{s}(r - 1) ,
$$

where the appropriate initial condition is $\bar{s}(0) = 0$. The solution to this recurrence can be shown to be $\bar{s}(r) - \mu(w, r)$ which is the expression given in corollary 4.4.1(a).

The expression for $\bar{s}_j(i)$ given in corollary 4.4.1(a) is consistent with the results obtained by C. S. Roberts (1979) who considered a retrieval technique based on weight-k superimposed code words. A summary of Roberts' work is given in Appendix B along with a derivation of the variance of the random variable that he considered. Corollary 4.4.1(b) can be seen to be a special case of this variance calculation.

4.3　Performance of Randomly Organized Files

We can now examine the expected behavior of randomly organized IDAM files. Recall from (4.6) that the expected number of accesses required to satisfy a query Q is given

$$
\bar{a}(Q) = \sum_{i=1}^{h} N_i \prod_{j \in Q} \frac{\bar{s}_j(i)}{w_j} .
$$

Note that we are ignoring the contribution of $\bar{a}_h(Q)$. From corollary 4.4.1(a) we have

$$
\bar{s}_j(i) = w_j \left[1 - \left(1 - \frac{1}{w_j} \right)^{r_i} \right] , \qquad (4.14)
$$

where

$$r_i = \prod_{k=0}^{i-1} b_k, \quad i > 0 \ (r_0 = 1)$$

is the number of records covered by a descriptor at level i. Therefore

$$\bar{a}(Q) = \sum_{i=1}^{h} N_i \prod_{j \in Q} \left[1 - \left(1 - \frac{1}{w_j} \right)^{r_i} \right].$$

Figure 4.1.

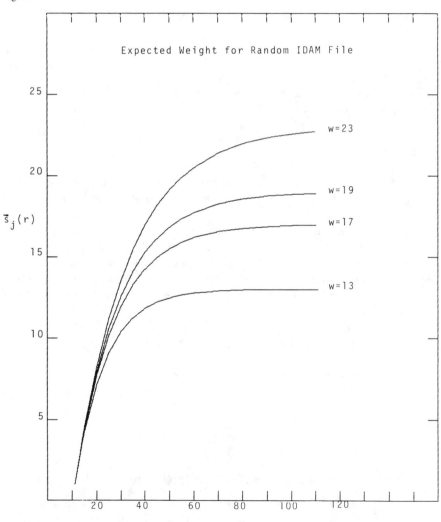

Expected Weight for Random IDAM File

Thus, the retrieval performance of randomly organized IDAM files is determined by the tree height, field widths, and blocking factors at each level in the tree as well as the number of attributes specified in a query.

Since we will often be interested in the behavior of $\bar{s}_j(i)$ as a function of r, the number of records covered by a descriptor, we will use the more descriptive notation $\bar{s}_j(r)$ and omit the subscript from r. When the field is unimportant we simply use $\bar{s}(r)$ to denote this quantity.

To understand more fully the effects of the various parameters on performance, we will look at (4.14) in more detail. Without loss of generality, we will consider a single field descriptor of width w covering r records. To simplify the discussion we will first derive an approximation to $\bar{s}(r)$. Since

$$\left(1 - \frac{1}{w} \right)^r \approx e^{-r/w}$$

as long as r/w^2 is small, we can approximate (4.14) by

$$\bar{s}(r) \approx w \left(1 - e^{-r/w} \right).$$

It can be seen from this expression that a field will saturate very rapidly as r increases. Figure 4.1 shows this effect on $\bar{s}(r)$ as r is increased. The only available control over this saturation is via the parameter w. That is, if a large r is anticipated, a correspondingly large width, w, will be required to achieve a desired level of retrieval performance.

Suppose for example that it is desired to maintain a field match probability of $\hat{p}$ at level i. Then we will want $1 - e^{-r/w} \leq \hat{p}$ or $r \leq -w \ln(1 - \hat{p})$. Thus, for a fixed probability $\hat{p}$, r is linear in w. That is, a large increase in r will require a proportional increase in w to maintain a fixed field match probability $\hat{p}$. Table 4.1 demonstrates the effect of increasing r on the field match probability $\rho(r)$. In the table is assumed that $\rho(r) \approx 1 - e^{-r/w}$.

Table 4.1.   Effects of Increasing r

r/w	$\rho(r)$
1	.63
2	.86
3	.95
4	.98
5	.99

Table 4.2.   Maximum Records Covered to Maintain $\hat{p} = .5$

$$r = w \ln 2 \approx .693w$$

w	r	$\rho(r)$	$\rho(r+1)$
5	3	.451	.551
10	6	.451	.503
15	10	.487	.519
20	13	.478	.503
25	17	.493	.513
30	20	.487	.503
35	24	.496	.510
40	27	.491	.503
45	31	.498	.509

Table 4.2 shows this effect for a fixed $\hat{p} = 0.5$. It can be seen from the table that doubling the number of records covered by a descriptor will require that the field width also be doubled to achieve the same field match probability.

We can conclude from this discussion that a random organization of IDAM files is acceptable for small files where very large descriptors may be tolerated. In very large files the descriptor storage overhead will become excessive. It should also be noted that large descriptors will require an increase in computational overhead to manage them.

5

D-trees over Sorted Files

We have seen that the behavior of *D*-trees over randomly organized files is completely determined by the tree height, field widths, and blocking factors at each level of the tree. It is natural now to ask the question: How can the retrieval performance of a *D*-tree be improved? As we shall see, the performance can be affected (indeed, quite radically) by an appropriate choice of data organization. In this chapter we will investigate the performance when the descriptors are sorted.

Sorted descriptor files can occur in two ways. First, the descriptors can be generated in the ordinary manner and subsequently sorted prior to building the *D*-tree. In this case, the physical correspondence between each level 0 descriptor and its associated data record must be explicitly preserved. Second, the data file itself can first be sorted and then order preserving transformations applied to produce a sorted *D*-tree.

In the subsequent analysis, we assume that the data file has been sorted with respect to the record descriptors where field 1 is taken to be the most significant sort key and field f the least significant. The sort order (ascending or descending) is not important.

5.1 Sorted Files of Descriptors

Recall from the last chapter that $\bar{s}_j(r)$ is the expected number of bits set in field j of a descriptor covering r records. In this section we present an informal discussion of the phenomena affecting $\bar{s}_j(r)$ when a file of descriptors is sorted.

Figure 5.1 shows a small sorted file of descriptors with format (4,4,4,4,4). In the figure we have grouped the descriptors according to the bit set in field 1. These breaks represent *transition* points in the field where one long run of bits terminates and another begins. Note the regular behavior of the leftmost fields. This may be attributed to the relatively low probability of a transition occurring. In contrast, the behavior in the rightmost fields is considerably more random owing to the increased probability of transitions occurring. We can therefore expect $\bar{s}_j(r)$ to be affected by this phenomenon.

Figure 5.1. Example of a Sorted Descriptor File

1	2	3	4	5
0001	0001	0001	0010	0001
0001	0001	0100	0010	0010
0001	0010	0100	0001	0001
0001	0010	0100	0010	0001
0001	0100	0100	0100	1000
0001	1000	0010	0100	0100
0001	1000	0100	0001	1000
0001	1000	0100	1000	0100
0010	0001	0010	0001	0001
0010	0010	0001	1000	0001
0010	0100	0100	1000	0001
0010	1000	0001	0100	1000
0010	1000	0100	0010	0001
0100	0001	0010	1000	0010
0100	0001	1000	0010	0100
0100	0100	0001	1000	1000
0100	0100	1000	0100	0100
1000	0010	0010	1000	0100
1000	0010	1000	0100	1000
1000	0100	0100	0100	0001

There are other effects that will play a role in the behavior of $\bar{s}_j(r)$. In figure 5.2(a), the first 20 records of a much larger file than that of figure 5.1 are shown. The effects observed in figure 5.1 have been magnified and can be clearly observed in figure 5.2(b). In figure 5.2(b) the column entries for field j have been suppressed after the first transition in field $j - 1$. The figure demonstrates that each field exhibits regular behavior to some extent, but over increasingly fewer descriptors as we move to the right. Thus, as more descriptors are grouped together in blocks, we can expect the behavior of the rightmost fields to become increasingly disordered.

We have observed that the probability of a transition occurring in field j will affect the quantity $\bar{s}_j(r)$. Notice, in fields 2 and 3 of figure 5.2(a), that the number of bits set in a block descriptor increases whenever a transition occurs. This is not true in fields 4 and 5. Here the probability of matching an existing bit in the block descriptor is increasing. The starred descriptors in Figure 5.2(a) illustrate this phenomenon. If we imagine the descriptors being entered into the file one at a time, the starred descriptors represent points at which a transition occurs, but the new bit matches some existing bit in the current block descriptor.

Figure 5.2. Transitions within Sorted Files

1	2	3	4	5		1	2	3	4	5
0001	0001	0001	0010	0001		0001	0001	0001	0010	0001
0001	0001	0001	0010	0010		0001	0001	0001	0010	0010
0001	0001	0001	1000	0001*		0001	0001	0001	1000	....
0001	0001	0010	0001	0010*		0001	0001	0010	....	....
0001	0001	0010	0001	0100		0001	0001	0010	....	....
0001	0001	0100	0001	0010		0001	0001	0100	....	....
0001	0001	0100	0010	0001		0001	0001	0100	....	....
0001	0010	0001	0100	0001		0001	0010	....	....	....
0001	0010	0010	0010	0001		0001	0010	....	....	....
0001	0010	0010	1000	0100		0001	0010	....	....	....
0001	0010	0100	0001	0001*		0001	0010	....	....	....
0001	0010	0100	0010*	0001		0001	0010	....	....	....
0001	0010	0100	0010	0010		0001	0010	....	....	....
0001	0010	0100	1000	1000		0001	0010	....	....	....
0001	0010	1000	0001	0001		0001	0010	....	....	....
0001	0010	1000	0100	1000*		0001	0010	....	....	....
0001	0100	0100	0100	1000		0001	0100	....	....	....
0001	0100	1000	1000	0010		0001	0100	....	....	....
0001	1000	0010	0010	1000*		0001	1000	....	....	....
0001	1000	0010	0100*	0100		0001	1000	....	....	....

(a)   (b)

We may infer from this discussion that the quantity $\bar{s}_j(r)$ will be affected by the probability of a transition occurring in field j and also by the probability of matching an existing bit in a field j of the block descriptor. The former effect is tending to increase $\bar{s}_j(r)$ while the latter is tending to limit the rate of increase.

We also note from figure 5.2(b) that a secondary effect is at play. That is, the probability of a transition occurring in field j is influenced by the probability of transitions in fields $1, 2, \ldots, j - 1$. For example, whenever a transition occurs in field $j - 1$, it is very likely that a transition to a low bit will occur in field j.

In the remainder of this chapter we will assess these effects in an effort to quantify $\bar{s}_j(r)$ for sorted D-trees.

5.2 Upper Bound on Bit Densities

In this section we present an upper bound for $\bar{s}_j(r)$ when a file of descriptors is sorted. We begin with some preliminary concepts necessary to prove the main result.

Let V be a set of m objects and let $(x_1, x_2, \ldots, x_n)$ be a sample of size n

where each $x_i \in V$ is drawn at random from V with replacement. Let U be the discrete random variable whose value is the number of distinct x_i in the n-tuple.

Lemma 5.1: U has pmf given by

$$Pr(U = t) = \frac{C_t^m \, S_t^n \, t!}{m^n}.$$

In particular, the expected value of U, denoted by $\bar{u}$, is given by

$$\bar{u} = m \left[1 - \left(1 - \frac{1}{m} \right)^n \right].$$

Proof: To find $Pr(U = t)$ we first note that there are C_t^m ways to choose the t distinct values. The n objects can be partitioned into exactly t nonempty subsets in S_t^n ways and the number of ways to distribute the t distinct values among the t subsets is $t!$. Thus, there are $C_t^m \, S_t^n \, t!$ samples (n-tuples) having precisely t distinct values. Since there are m^n total possible samples, it follows that

$$Pr(U = t) = \frac{C_t^m \, S_t^n \, t!}{m^n}.$$

This is the pmf of theorem 4.3 with parameters $w = m$ and $r = n$. Hence, from corollary 4.4.1(a) we have

$$\bar{u} = \mu(m,n) = m \left[1 - \left(1 - \frac{1}{m} \right)^n \right].$$

as the expected value of U. $\square$

Let us now consider a descriptor file at any level as a set of N f-tuples.

$$(v_{11}, \; v_{12}, \; ..., \; v_{1f})$$
$$(v_{21}, \; v_{22}, \; ..., \; v_{2f})$$
$$\cdot \qquad \cdot \qquad \cdot \qquad \cdot$$
$$\cdot \qquad \cdot \qquad \cdot \qquad \cdot$$
$$\cdot \qquad \cdot \qquad \cdot \qquad \cdot$$
$$(v_{N1}, \; v_{N2}, \; ..., \; v_{Nf})$$

If we (Codd 1970) project the file on the first j fields, we will obtain a file of, say, d, distinct j-tuples.

$$(v'_{11}, \; v'_{12}, \; ..., \; v'_{1j})$$
$$(v'_{21}, \; v'_{22}, \; ..., \; v'_{2j})$$
$$\cdot \qquad \cdot \qquad \cdot \qquad \cdot$$

$$\begin{matrix} . & & . & & . & & . \\ & . & & . & & . & & . \\ & & . & & . & & . \end{matrix}$$

$$(v'_{d1}, \quad v'_{d2}, \quad \ldots, \quad v'_{dj})$$

Let $\bar{d}_j$ denote the expected number of distinct j-tuples and let

$$v_j = \prod_{i=1}^{j} w_i$$

denote the volume of the space defined by the first j fields.

Theorem 5.2: Given that each v_{kj} is uniformly distributed on $[1, w_j]$ and the fields are independent, then $\bar{d}_j$ is given by

$$\bar{d}_j = v_j \left[1 - \left(1 - \frac{1}{v_j} \right)^N \right].$$

Proof: Since there are v_j possible distinct j-tuples, we can construct a 1-1 mapping from the j-tuples to the integers $1, 2, \ldots, v_j$. Under our assumptions, each of these integers will be equally likely. The result now follows from lemma 5.1 with $m = v_j$ and $n = N$. $\square$

Recall that when two adjacent descriptors in a file have different values in field j, we say that a *transition* occurs. That is, a transition occurs whenever $v_{kj} \neq v_{k+1, j}$. Let T_j denote the number of transitions occurring in field j of a sorted file of descriptors.

Lemma 5.3: Suppose that in a file of N descriptors there are d_j descriptors which are distinct in the first j fields. When this file of descriptors is sorted, $T_j \leq d_j - 1$.

Proof: Since we have d_j distinct j-tuples, we can partition the file into d_j classes. All the members of a class are identical and thus contain no transitions. In the worst case, each class will require the last field to distinguish it from the members of the next class in an ordering. Hence, at most $d_j - 1$ transitions will occur in the jth field. $\square$

The following result is an immediate consequence of lemma 5.3.

Corollary 5.3.1: Let $\bar{T}_j$ denote the expected number of transitions in the jth field of a sorted file of descriptors. Then $\bar{T}_j \leq \bar{d}_j - 1$.

Let t_j denote the probability of a transition occurring in the jth field between two consecutive descriptors. Since we expect $\bar{T}_j$ transitions and there are $N - 1$ locations within the file in which these transitions can occur, t_j is given by

$$t_j = \frac{\bar{T}_j}{N - 1}.$$

We are now ready to establish an upper bound on $\bar{s}_j(r)$. An obvious bound is

$$\bar{s}_j(r) \leqslant \min(r, w_j).$$

That is, we can have at most r bits set, but no more than all the bits can be set. In the following theorem we improve this bound.

Theorem 5.4: For sorted D-trees employing a weight-1 disjoint encoding method,

$$\bar{s}_j(r) \leqslant \begin{cases} 1 + (r - 1)t_j , & r \leqslant r' \\ \\ w_j & , r > r' \end{cases}$$

where

$$r' = 1 + \left\lfloor \frac{(w_j - 1)}{t_j} \right\rfloor$$

and

$$t_j = \frac{\bar{T}_j}{N - 1}$$

is the probability of a transition occurring in field j. Moreover, equality holds when $j = 1$ or when $r \leqslant 2$, that is,

(a) $\bar{s}_1(r) = 1 + (r - 1)t_1, \; 1 \leqslant r \leqslant N$ and
(b) $\bar{s}_j(r) = 1 + (r - 1)t_j, \; r \leqslant 2$.

Proof: To establish the bound we consider the worst case behavior, that is, we will assume that whenever a transition occurs within a block, the number of bits set will increase by one.

Let $X_j(r)$ be the discrete random variable denoting the number of bits set in field j of a block descriptor covering r records. Suppose we have a block of $r - 1$ descriptors with $X_j(r - 1)$ bits set in field j of the associated block descriptor. If we add a new descriptor to the block, under our worst case assumption the number of bits set will increase if a transition occurs. Thus,

$$X_j(r) = \begin{cases} X_j(r-1) & \text{w.p.} \ 1 - t_j \\ \\ X_j(r-1) + 1 & \text{w.p.} \ t_j \end{cases}$$

which gives rise to the recurrence

$$E[X_j(r)|X_j(r-1)] = X_j(r-1) + t_j.$$

Since $\bar{s}_j(r) = E[X_j(r)]$, taking the expectation of both sides we get the recurrence

$$\bar{s}_j(r) = \bar{s}_j(r-1) + t_j,$$

where the appropriate initial condition is $\bar{s}_j(1) = 1$. This recurrence has the solution

$$\bar{s}_j(r) = 1 + (r-1)t_j.$$

The bound now follows from the fact that we preclude the possibility of the new bit matching an existing bit.

We let r' be the largest integer satisfying the constraint $\bar{s}_j(r) \leqslant w_j$. This implies that $1 + (r-1)t_j \leqslant w_j$ or

$$r \leqslant 1 + \frac{(w_j - 1)}{t_j}.$$

Equality when $j = 1$ follows from the fact that in field 1 the number of bits set will always increase if a transition occurs, that is, the new bit will never match an existing bit. The case where $r = 1$ is immediate. Suppose that $r = 2$. Since there are only two descriptors in the block, it can never be the case that the new bit matches the existing bit when a transition occurs. $\square$

To make use of the bound given in theorem 5.4, we need to evaluate the transition probability, t_j. Since we can not evaluate $\bar{T}_j$ directly, the following corollary to the theorem gives a slightly coarser bound using an estimate of the transition probability for field j.

Corollary 5.4.1: For sorted D-trees employing a weight-1 disjoint encoding method,

$$\bar{s}_j(r) \leqslant \begin{cases} 1 + (r-1)\dfrac{\bar{d}_j - 1}{N - 1}, & r \leqslant r' \\ \\ w_j, & r > r' \end{cases}$$

where

$$r' = 1 + \left\lfloor \frac{(w_j - 1)(N - 1)}{\bar{d}_j - 1} \right\rfloor .$$

Proof: From corollary 5.3.1 we have $\bar{T}_j \leqslant \bar{d}_j - 1$. Thus,

$$t_j = \frac{\bar{T}_j}{N - 1} \leqslant \frac{\bar{d}_j - 1}{N - 1} .$$

The result now follows directly from theorem 5.4. □

As we will see, the bound of corollary 5.4.1 may be used as an estimator for $\bar{s}_j(r)$ when $N > \prod_{i=1}^{j} w_i$. This is usually the case in the higher order (leftmost) fields. However, as we move to the lower order fields, the bound increasingly overestimates $\bar{s}_j(r)$. This occurs because of our assumption that each transition will increase the number of bits set. Clearly, in the higher order fields where transitions occur relatively infrequently, this assumption is reasonable. However, in the lower order fields where transitions occur with increasing frequency, the probability of matching a bit which has already been set is also increasing. In this case the assumption is becoming less valid.

Thus, the bound can not be used as a "model" of the behavior of sorted D-trees. Specifically, as $j \rightarrow f$ (i.e., as we consider fields further to the right) the fields are becoming less ordered or alternatively, more random. This phenomenon is not captured in the behavior of the bound. That is, the bound suggests saturation, but not disorder.

Our intuitive expectation of the behavior of these files can be summarized as follows

(a) $\bar{s}_j(1, w_j, N) = 1$ (d) $\lim_{r \rightarrow N} \bar{s}_j(r, w_j, N) = w_j$

(b) $\bar{s}_j(r, 1, N) = 1$ (e) $\lim_{w_j \rightarrow \infty} \bar{s}_j(r, w_j, N) \leqslant r$

(c) $\bar{s}_j(r, w_j, 1) = 1$ (f) $\lim_{N \rightarrow \infty} \bar{s}_j(r, w_j, N) = 1$

Here we have explicitly shown the dependence of the bit density on the system parameters, r, w_j, N. In addition, we expect any expression for $\bar{s}_j (r, w_j, N)$ to reflect the increasing disorder of the fields as $j \rightarrow f$.

Before proceeding further, it will be instructive to examine the bound of corollary 5.4.1 in light of these properties. By inspection, properties (a) and (b) are satisfied. Property (c) is also satisfied since $r \leqslant N$ implies that $r = 1$ when $N = 1$. Property (d) is only satisfied by the restriction $r \leqslant r'$ (see the corollary). It can be shown that as $w_j \rightarrow \infty$ the bound approaches r so that property (e) is satisfied.

As

$$N \to \infty, \bar{d}_j \to \prod_{i=1}^{f} w_i,$$

a constant, therefore property (f) is also satisfied.

As we have observed, the problems exhibited by the bound as a model of the behavior of sorted *D*-trees stem from the assumption that each transition within a block will cause a new bit to be set. This is clearly true in field 1, but becomes increasingly violated as we move to the lower order fields where a new bit is more likely to match an existing bit in the block descriptor. This observation suggests a more refined model for the behavior of sorted *D*-trees which is discussed in the next section.

5.3   A First Order Model of Behavior

Again let $X_j(r)$ denote the number of bits set in field j of a block descriptor covering r records. Suppose that we have a block of $r - 1$ descriptors with $X_j(r - 1)$ bits set in field j of the block descriptor and we add a new descriptor to the block. The number of bits in the block descriptor will increase by one if we have a transition in field j *and* the new bit does not match an existing bit. The number of bits will remain the same if either: (1) we do not have a transition; or (2) we have a transition and the new bit matches an existing bit.

To formalize this model let us consider the jth field of a block of $r - 1$ descriptors as a sequence of integers, $\langle x_1, x_2, \ldots, x_{r-2}, x_{r-1} \rangle$, where $x_i, 1 \leqslant x_i \leqslant w_j$, denotes the number of the bit set in the field. Now suppose that we add a new descriptor with bit x_r set in field j. Let t_j denote the probability of a transition, that is,

$$t_j = Pr(x_r \neq x_{r-1}).$$

Let m_j denote the probability of matching some other bit, that is,

$$m_j = Pr(x_r = x_k, \text{for some } k = 1, 2, \ldots, r - 2).$$

We can now state the model as

$$X_j(r) = \begin{cases} X_j(r - 1) & \text{w.p.} \quad t_j m_j + (1 - t_j) \\ X_j(r - 1) + 1 & \text{w.p.} \quad t_j(1 - m_j) \end{cases}$$

where we have assumed the independence of the probabilities t_j and m_j.

The upper bound of theorem 5.4 was derived by assuming that $m_j = 0$. Let us now assume that given a transition, the new bit is equally likely to match an existing bit, and since there are $X_j(r - 2)$ bits set in the block descriptor for the first $r - 2$ records, we can denote the probability of this event by

$$m_j = \frac{X_j(r - 2)}{w_j} .$$

Later we will question these assumptions, specifically as they relate to the application of this model to sorted files of descriptors.

Substituting into the model and taking expectations yields the recurrence

$$\bar{s}_j(r) = \bar{s}_j(r - 1) + t_j \left(1 - \frac{\bar{s}_j(r - 2)}{w_j} \right) \tag{5.1}$$

where the appropriate initial conditions are

$$\bar{s}_j(0) = 0 \text{ and } \bar{s}_j(1) = 1. \tag{5.2}$$

Theorem 5.5: Given the conditions of the preceding model, if $w_j \geq 4$ (or $t_j \leq w_j/4$), then

$$\bar{s}_j(r) = w_j - \left(\frac{w_j(1+\alpha)-2}{2\alpha} \right) \left(\frac{1+\alpha}{2} \right)^r + \left(\frac{w_j(1-\alpha)-2}{2\alpha} \right) \left(\frac{1-\alpha}{2} \right)^r$$

where

$$\alpha = \left(1 - 4 \frac{t_j}{w_j} \right)^{1/2} .$$

Proof: Note that $w_j \geq 4$ implies that $t_j \leq \frac{w_j}{4}$.

This latter condition is sufficient and may be true even in cases where $w_j < 4$.

The expression given by the theorem results from the solution of recurrence (5.1). We first show that the initial conditions (5.2) are satisfied and then complete the proof by induction on r.

$$\bar{s}_j(0) = w_j - \left(\frac{w_j(1+\alpha)-2}{2\alpha} \right) + \left(\frac{w_j(1-\alpha)-2}{2\alpha} \right)$$

$$= w_j - \frac{2w_j\alpha}{2\alpha} = 0$$

$$\bar{s}_j(1) = w_j - \left(\frac{w_j(1+\alpha)-2}{2\alpha} \right) \left(\frac{1+\alpha}{2} \right) + \left(\frac{w_j(1-\alpha)-2}{2\alpha} \right) \left(\frac{1-\alpha}{2} \right)$$

$$= w_j - \frac{w_j(1+\alpha)^2}{4\alpha} + \frac{1+\alpha}{2\alpha} + \frac{w_j(1-\alpha)^2}{4\alpha} - \frac{1-\alpha}{2\alpha}$$

$$= w_j - \frac{w_j + 2w_j\alpha + w_j\alpha^2}{4\alpha} + \frac{w_j - 2w_j\alpha + w_j\alpha^2}{4\alpha} + 1$$

$$= w_j - \frac{4w_j\alpha}{4\alpha} + 1 = 1.$$

Thus, the initial conditions are satisfied. Now, as the inductive hypothesis, assume that the theorem holds for $r \leqslant k - 1$. We want to show that it also holds for $r = k$. We first let

$$\bar{s}_j(r) = w_j - c_1 \left(\frac{1+\alpha}{2} \right)^r + c_2 \left(\frac{1-\alpha}{2} \right)^r,$$

where the c_i are constants independent of r. From recurrence (5.1) we have

$$\bar{s}_j(k) = \bar{s}_j(k - 1) + t_j \left(1 - \frac{\bar{s}_j(k - 2)}{w_j} \right)$$

$$= \bar{s}_j(k - 1) - \frac{t_j}{w_j} \bar{s}_j(k - 2) + t_j .$$

Hence, by the inductive hypothesis,

$$\bar{s}_j(k) = w_j - c_1 \left(\frac{1+\alpha}{2} \right)^{k-1} + c_2 \left(\frac{1-\alpha}{2} \right)^{k-1}$$

$$- \frac{t_j}{w_j} \left[w_j - c_1 \left(\frac{1+\alpha}{2} \right)^{k-2} + c_2 \left(\frac{1-\alpha}{2} \right)^{k-2} \right] + t_j$$

$$= w_j - c_1 \left[\left(\frac{1+\alpha}{2} \right)^{k-1} - \frac{t_j}{w_j} \left(\frac{1+\alpha}{2} \right)^{k-2} \right]$$

$$+ c_2 \left[\left(\frac{1-\alpha}{2} \right)^{k-1} - \frac{t_j}{w_j} \left(\frac{1-\alpha}{2} \right)^{k-2} \right]$$

$$= w_j - c_1 \left[\frac{2}{1+\alpha} - \frac{t_j}{w_j} \left(\frac{2}{1+\alpha} \right)^2 \right] \left(\frac{1+\alpha}{2} \right)^k$$

$$+ c_2 \left[\frac{2}{1-\alpha} - \frac{t_j}{w_j} \left(\frac{2}{1-\alpha} \right)^2 \right] \left(\frac{1-\alpha}{2} \right)^k$$

$$= w_j - c_1 \left[\frac{2w_j(1+\alpha) - 4t_j}{w_j(1+\alpha)^2} \right] \left(\frac{1+\alpha}{2} \right)^k$$

$$+ c_2 \left[\frac{2w_j(1-\alpha) - 4t_j}{w_j(1-\alpha)^2} \right] \left(\frac{1-\alpha}{2} \right)^k .$$

Now consider the denominator the first term in brackets.

$$w_j(1 + \alpha)^2 = w_j(1 + 2\alpha + a^2)$$

$$= w_j(1 + 2\alpha + 1 - 4t_j/w_j) = 2w_j(1 + \alpha) - 4t_j.$$

Similarly, the denominator of the second term in brackets is

$$w_j(1 - \alpha)^2 = w_j(1 - 2\alpha + \alpha^2)$$

$$= w_j(1 - 2\alpha + 1 - 4t_j/w_j) = 2w_j(1 - \alpha) - 4t_j.$$

Therefore, both terms in brackets equal one and we are left with

$$\bar{s}_j(k) = w_j - c_1 \left(\frac{1+\alpha}{2}\right)^k + c_2 \left(\frac{1-\alpha}{2}\right)^k,$$

and thus the theorem holds for $r = k$. $\square$

Thus far we have not considered the effects of t_j on the model. The proofs of the next two corollaries to theorem 5.5 are straightforward and are given in Appendix C. The following result helps to characterize the model for specific choices of the transition probability, t_j.

Corollary 5.5.1: Two special cases of theorem 5.5 are

(a) $\bar{s}_j(r) = 1$ $\qquad\qquad$ $t_j = 0$

(b) $\bar{s}_j(r) = w_j\left(1 - t_j^r\right)$ $\qquad$ $t_j = 1 - \dfrac{1}{w_j}$.

Corollary 5.5.1(a) corresponds to the constant model while corollary 5.5.1(b) is the random model (cf. corollary 4.4.1) of chapter 4. Thus if t_j increases as $j \to f$, the behavior of the fields will tend toward the random model.

The next result characterizes the asymptotic behavior of the model.

Corollary 5.5.2: Let $\bar{s}_j(r, w_j)$ denote the expression in theorem 5.5.

(a) $\displaystyle\lim_{r \to \infty} \bar{s}_j(r, w_j) = \begin{cases} 1 & , \alpha = 1 \\ \\ w_j, & \alpha < 1 \end{cases}$

(b) $\displaystyle\lim_{w_j \to \infty} \bar{s}_j(r, w_j) = 1 + (r - 1)t_j.$

The corollary accords well with our intuitive expectation. Note from corollary 5.5.2(b) that as the field width increases, the model of theorem 5.5 is approaching the bound of theorem 5.4.

As in the case of theorem 5.4, in subsequent approximations to $\bar{s}_j(r)$ using the model of theorem 5.5. for sorted *D*-trees, we use

$$\frac{\bar{d}_j - 1}{N - 1}$$

as an estimate of the transition probability, t_j, in field j. For this choice of t_j note from corollary 5.5.2(b), that the model of theorem 5.5 approaches the upper bound of corollary 5.4.1 as w_j gets large.

To understand more fully the factors influencing the saturation of the high order fields in sorted descriptor files, and thus be in a position to control this saturation if possible, we need to examine the model of theorem 5.5 more closely. This is most easily done by considering an approximation to the model. In Appendix D it is shown that when $4t_j/w_j$ is small, the model of theorem 5.5 can be approximated by

$$\bar{s}_j(r) = 1 + (r - 1)\left(1 - \frac{1}{w_j}\right)t_j + \frac{t_j}{w_j} + O\left(\frac{t_j^2}{w_j^2}\right). \tag{5.4}$$

It is clear from equation (5.4) that the expected bit density is influenced by two factors: (1) the transition probability; and (2) the width of the field. It should therefore be possible to impede the saturation of a field by either reducing the transition probability or by increasing the field width. Unfortunately, these two goals are incompatible and cannot be simultaneously achieved. To see this, note from theorem 5.2 that as w_j is allowed to increase without bound, $\bar{d}_j \to N$ which implies that $t_j \to 1$. This is somewhat mitigated by the fact that as $t_j \to 1$ we have from theorem 5.4 that $\bar{s}_j(r) \to r$. Now recall that the probability of matching in field j is given by

$$\rho_j(r) = \frac{\bar{s}_j(r)}{w_j},$$

so that when w_j is allowed to increase without bound,

$$\rho_j(r) \to \frac{r}{w_j} \to 0.$$

Therefore, even though the transition probability increases, the probability of matching in field j will decrease.

We can make two further observations about the relationship of the model of theorem 5.5 to theorem 5.4 by examining equation (5.4) in more detail. First, note that when N is large with respect to v_j we have

$$t_j = \frac{v_j - 1}{N - 1} \approx \frac{v_j}{N} .$$

Since

$$v_j = \prod_{i=1}^{j} w_j = w_j v_{j-1}$$

we have

$$\frac{t_j}{w_j} \approx \frac{v_j}{w_j N} = \frac{v_{j-1}}{N} = t_{j-1}$$

Thus, equation (5.4) is approximately

$$\bar{s}_j \approx 1 + (r - 1)\left(1 - \frac{1}{w_j}\right)t_j + t_{j-1} + O\left(t_{j-2^2}\right).$$

$$= 1 + (r - 1)t_j - (r - 2)t_{j-1} + O\left(t_{j-2^2}\right) . \tag{5.5}$$

Equation (5.5) shows clearly that the expected number of bits set in field j is influenced not only by the transition probability in field j, but also by the transition probabilities in fields $1, 2, \ldots, j - 1$. So the model incorporates this secondary effect at least to some degree.

We also note from equation (5.5) that the model of theorem 5.5. is very close to the bound of theorem 5.4 when t_j is small, that is, in the high order fields. Indeed, since $t_0 = 0$, they will give approximately the same values for field 1.

5.4   Estimating Expected Weights for Sorted Files

We have established an upper bound on $\bar{s}_j(r)$, the expected number of bits set in field j of a sorted files of descriptors containing r descriptors per block. In addition, we have proposed a first order model for the behavior of sorted files. We now turn to the issue of estimating $\bar{s}_j(r)$. In particular, we will assess the adequacy of the bound of theorem 5.4 and the model of theorem 5.5 when making such estimates. Although this discussion will center around a specific example, the observations are more generally applicable.

For this particular example, we chose a descriptor containing five fields of $w_j = 10$ $(1 \leqslant j \leqslant 5)$ bits each and examined files of $N = 50,000$ records. Descriptors were generated randomly by selecting five integers uniformly from $[1,10]$. These integers determined the particular bit set in each field of the descriptor. After generating 50,000 descriptors in this manner, the file was sorted. The sorted file was then blocked into groups of r records and the average number of bits set in each field of the resulting block descriptors was calculated. The number of records, r, covered by a block descriptor was varied from 1 to 100. This procedure was repeated five times and the resulting observations were used to construct 99.5 percent confidence intervals for the unknown parameter $\bar{s}_j(r)$. The results of this experiment are summarized in table 5.1 where each entry is the 99.5 percent confidence interval for $\bar{s}_j(r)$.

It can be seen from table 5.1 that even these very conservative confidence intervals are quite small ($< \pm.06$) indicating that the experiment was sufficiently precise to remove much of the "noise" in the observations. The data of table 5.1 was plotted and is shown in figure 5.3 where the curves pass through the center of the confidence intervals. We have connected the points for visual clarity even though $\bar{s}_j(r)$ is not a continuous function of r.

We see from figure 5.3 that the high order fields (1, 2 and 3) are experiencing a gradual linear rate of saturation while the low order fields (4 and 5) are saturating at an exponential rate. This fact is directly attributable to the increasing disorder in the low order fields compared to the relative regular behavior of the high order fields.

The upper bounds on $\bar{s}_j(r)$ given by theorem 5.4 are shown along with the observed data in figure 5.4. Note the close agreement between the bound and the observations particularly in the fields where $N > \nu_j$. In fact within the resolution of the plotter used, the first three fields are exactly predicted by the upper bound. This results because when $N > \nu_j$, the assumption underlying the derivation of the upper bound (that is, whenever a transition occurs, a new bit is set in the block descriptor) is most nearly true. The agreement is less precise in the low order fields where the bound becomes increasingly conservative.

It is clear from figure 5.4 that the upper bound of theorem 5.4 may reliably be used to estimate $\bar{s}_j(r)$ under certain conditions, specifically when $N > \nu_j$. We now examine the model of theorem 5.5. for its potential as an estimator. Figure 5.5 shows the observations together with the values calculated from the theorem using the estimated value for t_j. The agreement is close in fields 1, 2 and 5, while the model is too low in fields 3 and 4. The close agreement in the first two fields is expected since as we have already noted (cf. equation 5.5), theorem 5.4 and theorem 5.5 yield approximately the same values when the transition probability, t_j, is very small. The agreement in the last field results from the relatively large transition probability or equivalently the increased disorder. Recall from corollary 5.5.1(b) that as the transition probability increases, the behavior of the field approaches the behavior of a randomly organized file.

We assumed in the formulation of the model leading to theorem 5.5 that when a transition occurred, the new bit was equally likely to match one of the existing bits. The empirical evidence presented here serves to cast further doubt on this assumption and in addition suggests that there are situations in which it is not even

Table 5.1. Observed $\bar{s}_j(r)$ for Sorted Descriptor File

r	Field 1	2	3	4	5
1	1.000 ± .000	1.000 ± .000	1.000 ± .000	1.000 ± .000	1.000 ± .000
2	1.000 ± .000	1.002 ± .000	1.020 ± .002	1.198 ± .005	1.784 ± .005
3	1.000 ± .000	1.004 ± .000	1.041 ± .002	1.396 ± .005	2.550 ± .006
4	1.000 ± .000	1.006 ± .001	1.060 ± .003	1.598 ± .007	3.283 ± .010
5	1.001 ± .000	1.008 ± .001	1.080 ± .003	1.796 ± .011	3.958 ± .012
10	1.002 ± .001	1.018 ± .001	1.179 ± .005	2.788 ± .021	6.438 ± .045
15	1.003 ± .000	1.028 ± .002	1.280 ± .006	3.785 ± .012	7.892 ± .041
20	1.003 ± .000	1.038 ± .001	1.379 ± .005	4.776 ± .030	8.762 ± .037
25	1.004 ± .001	1.048 ± .002	1.478 ± .005	5.763 ± .021	9.261 ± .025
30	1.005 ± .000	1.058 ± .002	1.580 ± .009	6.762 ± .030	9.567 ± .014
35	1.006 ± .001	1.067 ± .002	1.680 ± .006	7.738 ± .043	9.742 ± .028
40	1.007 ± .000	1.078 ± .001	1.778 ± .006	8.624 ± .059	9.855 ± .024
45	1.008 ± .000	1.087 ± .004	1.879 ± .006	9.303 ± .015	9.909 ± .007
50	1.009 ± .001	1.097 ± .003	1.977 ± .016	9.709 ± .033	9.947 ± .019
60	1.011 ± .000	1.118 ± .002	2.180 ± .008	9.947 ± .008	9.980 ± .010
70	1.012 ± .001	1.136 ± .004	2.379 ± .013	9.973 ± .013	9.993 ± .010
80	1.014 ± .000	1.158 ± .002	2.578 ± .016	9.987 ± .005	9.998 ± .004
90	1.016 ± .000	1.177 ± .005	2.780 ± .014	9.993 ± .005	10.00 ± .002
100	1.017 ± .002	1.195 ± .006	2.976 ± .016	9.999 ± .002	10.00 ± .002

Figure 5.3.

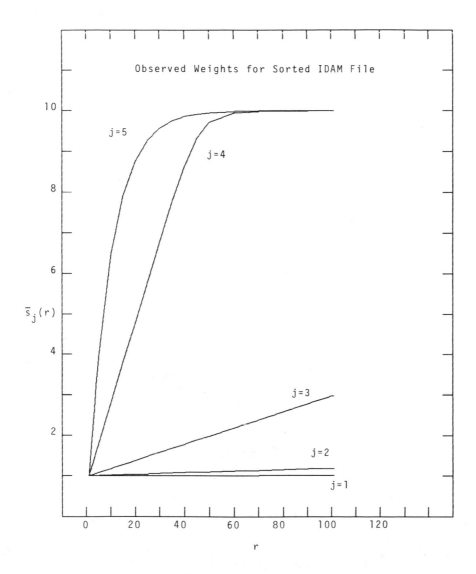

a good approximation. The evidence does suggest, however, that the model of theorem 5.5 is a lower bound on $\bar{s}_j(r)$. As a rule of thumb, theorem 5.5 gives a good estimate of the actual behavior when $N < \nu_j$.

To summarize, the models of behavior developed in the last section may be

Figure 5.4.

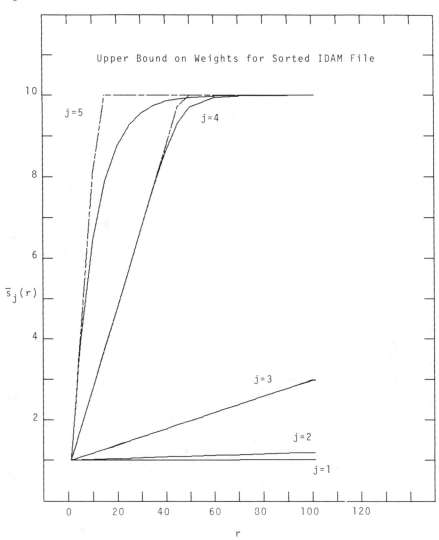

used to reasonably predict the actual behavior of sorted *D*-trees. The best estimates of behavior result when:

1. $N > \nu_j$: $\bar{s}_j(r)$ is estimated by theorem 5.4.
2. $N < \nu_j$: $\bar{s}_j(r)$ is estimated by theorem 5.5.

Using this criterion, fields 1 though 3 of our example are best estimated by theorem 5.4 while field 5 is best estimated by theorem 5.5. This is graphically

Figure 5.5.

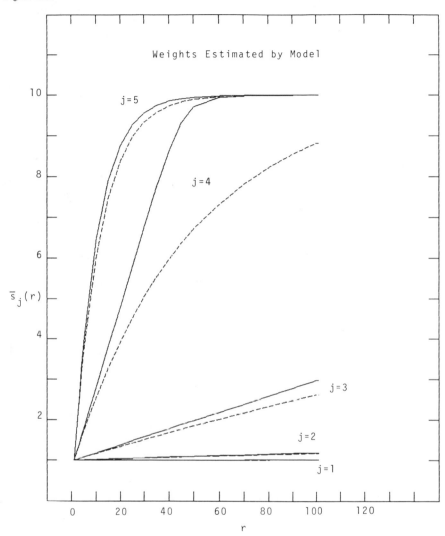

depicted in figure 5.6. These estimates are quite close and are certainly adequate to assess retrieval performance.

5.5 Discussion of Model Error

It is evident from figure 5.5 that the model of theorem 5.5 is of limited value in estimating $\bar{s}_j(r)$ for sorted D-trees. To understand why the model gives estimates which are too low in the interior fields (especially field 4) we need to examine

Figure 5.6.

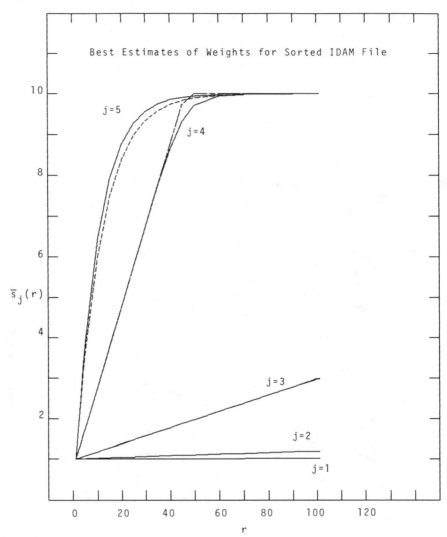

it more closely. There are three possible areas in which the model could be deficient: (1) violation of the independence assumption for t_j and m_j; (2) estimation of t_j; and (3) estimation of m_j. The influence of any or all of these factors could lead to the low estimates for $\bar{s}_j(r)$ observed in figure 5.5. We will briefly discuss each of these areas.

In deriving the model of theorem 5.5, we assumed that the probability of matching an existing bit was independent of the probability that a transition had occurred.

Figure 5.7.   File of Figure 5.2(a) Revisited

1	2	3	4	5
0001	0001	0001	0010	0001
0001	0001	0001	0010	0010
0001	0001	0001	1000	0001
0001	0001	0010	0001	0010
0001	0001	0010	0001	0100
0001	0001	0100	0001	0010
0001	0001	0100	0010	0001
0001	0010	0001	0100	0001
0001	0010	0010	0010	0001
0001	0010	0010	1000	0100
0001	0010	0100	0001	0001
0001	0010	0100	0010	0001
0001	0010	0100	0010	0010
0001	0010	0100	1000	1000
0001	0010	1000	0001	0001
0001	0010	1000	0100	1000
0001	0100	0100	0100	1000
0001	0100	1000	1000	0010
0001	1000	0010	0010	1000
0001	1000	0010	0100	0100

This is clearly not true for sorted D trees. To see this, consider again the file of descriptors shown in figure 5.2(a). For convenience this file is shown in figure 5.7. It is clear from field 2 of the file that the probability of matching an existing bit given that a transition has occurred is 0. Similarly, the probability of matching an existing bit given that a transition has not occurred is 1. In field 5 however, the situation is quite different. Due to the extreme variability in the locations of the bits, it seems that here the assumption is more nearly true. Whatever the effects due to the violation of the independence assumption, they should be most pronounced in the high order fields. To eliminate them altogether, the probabilities, m_j, in the model should therefore more properly be conditioned on the transition probability, t_j.

We now consider the effects of the estimation of t_j and m_j on the model. The model states that when a new descriptor is added to a block, the number of bits set in the block descriptor will increase if:

1. a transitions occurs; *and*
2. the new bit does not match an existing bit in the sub-block of $(r - 2)$ descriptors formed by deleting descriptors r and $r - 1$.

We may conclude that the model will be unnecessarily low if either:

1. the estimate of the transition probability is too low; or
2. the estimate of the probability of matching an existing bit is too high.

Recall that our estimate of the transition probability, t_j, is given by

$$\frac{\bar{d}_j - 1}{N - 1} \tag{5.6}$$

where

$$\bar{d}_j = v_j \left[1 - \left(1 - \frac{1}{v_j} \right)^N \right] \quad \text{and} \quad v_j = \prod_{i=1}^{j} w_i \,.$$

We have already asserted that (5.6) overestimates the true transition probability. For the example of the last section, we can determine confidence bounds on the true transition probability from the data in table 5.1 as follows. From theorem 5.4 we have

$$\bar{s}_j(r) = 1 + (r - 1)t_j, \quad r \leqslant 2.$$

Therefore, $\bar{s}_j(2) = 1 + t_j$, or alternatively,

$$t_j = \bar{s}_j(2) - 1. \tag{5.7}$$

The model of theorem 5.5 also predicts this value for $\bar{s}_j(2)$. This is most easily verified by inspection of the underlying recurrence relation. From equations (5.1) and (5.2) we have

$$\bar{s}_j(r) = \bar{s}_j(r - 1) + t_j \left(1 - \frac{\bar{s}_j(r - 2)}{w_j} \right)$$

with initial conditions $\bar{s}_j(0) = 0$ and $\bar{s}_j(1) = 1$. Hence, $\bar{s}_j(2) = 1 + t_j$.

We can therefore use the observations for $r = 2$ in table 5.1 and equation (5.7) to calculate confidence bounds for the true transition probability. Table 5.2 shows the results of these calculations along with our estimate of t_j from equation (5.6).

Table 5.2. Transition Probabilities t_j

_j_	Estimated	Observed
1	0.00018	0.00015 ± .00009
2	0.00198	0.00190 ± .00046
3	0.01998	0.01964 ± .00158
4	0.19864	0.19822 ± .00480
5	0.78694	0.78408 ± .00498

As can be seen from the table, equation (5.6) gives estimates of t_j which are slightly higher than the observed mean value. This agrees with our prior assertion that equation (5.6) overestimates the true transition probability. Note however that the data does not contradict the hypothesis that the true transition probability has the value given by equation (5.6). It seems clear that the estimate of the transition probability is not the source of the conservative nature of the model of theorem 5.5. We are forced to conclude that either the probability of matching an existing bit, m_j, is too high or the effects due to the violation of the independence assumption are greater than anticipated.

Any influence due to an inappropriate choice of m_j should be most pronounced in the interior fields. Consider the term

$$t_j \left(1 - \frac{\bar{s}_j(r-2)}{w_j} \right)$$

in recurrence 5.1. In the higher order fields, the transition probability is quite small, but so is the probability of matching an existing bit. Therefore the contribution of this term will be correspondingly small. This will tend to minimize any effects due to the violation of the independence assumption or the choice of m_j.

In the low order fields the transition probability is large, but the probability of matching an existing bit is also large. In fact, here the assumption that a new bit is equally likely to match an existing bit, is most nearly true. These factors should tend to offset one another.

It seems likely that the choice of m_j in the model of theorem 5.5 is chiefly responsible for the underestimation of $\bar{s}_j(r)$ observed in figure 5.5. However, it is unclear how the violation of the independence assumption will manifest itself.

Although the model of theorem 5.5 is of limited value in estimating $\bar{s}_j(r)$ for the interior fields of sorted D-trees, it is still a useful result. For example, it could have been used to deduce $\bar{s}_j(r)$ for the randomly organized files of chapter 4 (compare corollary 5.5.1(b) with corollary 4.4.1(a)). It may also be useful in the analysis of other IDAM organizations for which the assumptions are satisfied. Empirical evidence suggests that the model of theorem 5.5 is a lower bound for $\bar{s}_j(r)$ when descriptor files are sorted.

In the example of the next section, we will show the values predicted by the model as well as those from the upper bound. This should lend credence to our conjecture. Since we have no desire to artificially improve the performance of sorted IDAM files, we will use the upper bound of theorem 5.4 when estimating this performance in subsequent chapters.

5.6   Retrieval Performance—An Example

There has only been one instance of a sorted IDAM file reported in the literature (Pfaltz, Berman and Cagley 1980). This file consists of 1.44 million data records sorted and indexed on seven fields. A 70-bit descriptor divided into seven 10-bit fields is used for storage and retrieval. The data file is organized into 60,000 blocks containing 24 records each. Two index levels are used with an index blocking factor of 128 descriptors per block.

The block descriptors in the level 1 index cover $r = 24$ records while those in the level 2 index cover $r = 24 \times 128 = 3072$ data records. Using these values for r, we can calculate an upper bound for $\bar{s}_j(r)$ from corollary 5.4.1 and also the values of $\bar{s}_j(r)$ given by the model of theorem 5.5 using

$$\frac{\bar{d}_j - 1}{N - 1}$$

as an estimate for t_j, the transition probability in field j. Table 5.3(a) shows the results of these calculations. These values accord well with the observations given in Pfaltz, Berman and Cagley's Table I.

It can be seen that the last two fields in the level 1 index are quite saturated while the last four fields of the level 2 index are essentially saturated. Indeed, the last three fields of the level 2 index are almost certain to be completely saturated. We have already noted that there are two ways to control the saturation of low order fields in sorted D-trees: (1) by increasing the field widths; or (2) by reducing the transition probabilities. We have also observed that these are incompatible goals. In table 5.3(b) and table 5.3(c) the values are shown when the last three field widths have been increased to 50 and 100 respectively. Note that $\bar{s}_j(r)$, $1 \leqslant j \leqslant 4$ is unchanged. This is to be expected since the number of data records

Table 5.3. $\bar{s}_j(r)$ for Sorted D-trees

$(10,10,10,10,10,10,10)$

24		1.000	1.001	1.014	1.143	2.347	7.625	9.278
	ub	1.000	1.002	1.016	1.160	2.597	10.000	10.000
3072		1.017	1.188	2.727	8.936	10.000	10.000	10.000
	ub	1.019	1.211	3.131	10.000	10.000	10.000	10.000

(a)

$(10,10,10,10,50,50,50)$

24		1.000	1.001	1.014	1.143	7.924	19.087	19.502
	ub	1.000	1.002	1.016	1.160	8.538	23.350	23.987
3072		1.017	1.188	2.727	8.936	50.000	50.000	50.000
	ub	1.019	1.211	3.131	10.000	50.000	50.000	50.000

(b)

$(10,10,10,10,100,100,100)$

24		1.000	1.001	1.014	1.143	12.448	21.485	21.617
	ub	1.000	1.002	1.016	1.160	13.188	23.835	23.998
3072		1.017	1.188	2.727	8.936	100.000	100.000	100.000
	ub	1.019	1.211	3.131	10.000	100.000	100.000	100.000

(c)

$(5,5,5,5,5,5,5)$

24		1.000	1.000	1.002	1.008	1.040	1.197	1.905
	ub	1.000	1.000	1.002	1.010	1.050	1.250	2.248
3072		1.007	1.041	1.206	1.935	3.946	4.995	5.000
	ub	1.009	1.051	1.264	2.331	5.000	5.000	5.000

(d)

N has not changed. Notice that an effect on the level 1 index has been achieved while no improvement in the level 2 index has been attained. It can be seen from the last two fields in the level 1 index ($r = 24$) that $s_j(r) \to 24$ as expected. Thus,

$$\rho_j(r) = \frac{\bar{s}_j(r)}{w_j}$$

is decreasing rapidly with increasing field width. For comparison, the $\rho_j(r)$ are shown in table 5.4.

The second way to lower $\bar{s}_j(r)$ is to reduce the transition probability in field j. This can only be accomplished by reducing v_j, the size of the space defined by the first j fields. The size of the space can only be reduced by decreasing some or all of the widths in fields $1, 2, \ldots , j$. Table 5.3(d) shows the values obtained for the expected number of bits set when all the field widths have been reduced to five bits. It can be seen that $\bar{s}_j(r)$ has been reduced quite significantly. However, since

$$\rho_j(r) \geqslant \frac{1}{w_j},$$

we see from table 5.4(d) that the probability of matching the low order fields has been reduced at the expense of increasing the probability of matching the high order fields. Notice also that some marginal improvement in the level 2 index has been achieved.

In summary, the effect of increasing the field widths is to gain some sensitivity in the level 1 index at the expense of increased storage. Reducing the size of the space increases the sensitivity in the low order fields at the expense of the higher order fields achieving a more balanced retrieval structure. At the same time, reducing the size of the space will lower the overall storage overhead of the index files.

To get a feel for the effects of these changes on retrieval performance, we have calculated the expected number of accesses necessary to respond to a fully qualified (i.e., all fields specified) query for each of the descriptor formats shown in table 5.3. Recall from equation (4.6) that this is given by

$$\sum_{i=1}^{h} N_i \prod_{j=1}^{f} \rho_j(r_i)$$

where N_i is the number of entries at level i and r_i is the number of data records covered by a descriptor at level i. The upper bound and the value predicted by the model of theorem 5.5 for the expected number of accesses are shown in table 5.5.

The effect of increasing the field widths in the low order fields is to reduce the expected number of accesses by approximately one access, while reducing the size of the space increases the expected number of accesses by approximately one access. The expected retrieval performance for a fully qualified query is essentially unchanged when the low order field widths are doubled from 50 to 100 bits.

Table 5.4. $p_j(r)$ for Sorted D-trees

(10,10,10,10,10,10,10)

24		.1000	.1001	.1014	.1143	.2347	.7625	.9278
	ub	.1000	.1002	.1016	.1160	.2597	1.0000	1.0000
3072		.1017	.1188	.2727	.8936	1.0000	1.0000	1.0000
	ub	.1019	.1211	.3131	1.0000	1.0000	1.0000	1.0000

(a)

(10,10,10,10,50,50,50)

24		.1000	.1001	.1014	.1143	.1585	.3817	.3900
	ub	.1000	.1002	.1016	.1160	.1708	.4670	.4797
3072		.1017	.1188	.2727	.8936	1.0000	1.0000	1.0000
	ub	.1019	.1211	.3131	1.0000	1.0000	1.0000	1.0000

(b)

(10,10,10,10,100,100,100)

24		.1000	.1001	.1014	.1143	.1245	.2148	.2162
	ub	.1000	.1002	.1016	.1160	.1319	.2384	.2400
3072		.1017	.1188	.2727	.8936	1.0000	1.0000	1.0000
	ub	.1019	.1211	.3131	1.0000	1.0000	1.0000	1.0000

(c)

(5,5,5,5,5,5,5)

24		.2000	.2001	.2003	.2016	.2080	.2395	.3809
	ub	.2000	.2001	.2004	.2020	.2100	.2499	.4496
3072		.2014	.2081	.2412	.3870	.7891	.9990	1.0000
	ub	.2017	.2102	.2529	.4662	1.0000	1.0000	1.0000

(d)

Table 5.5.   The Expected Number of Accesses for a
Fully Qualified Query

Descriptor Format	Model (5.5)	Upper Bound
(10,10,10,10,10,10,10)	3.5	4.7
(10,10,10,10,50,50,50)	2.5	3.1
(10,10,10,10,100,100,100)	2.4	2.9
(5,5,5,5,5,5,5)	4.3	5.6

Table 5.5 shows that the expected retrieval performance for a fully qualified query is reasonable even for the small (35-bit) descriptor. It appears from the data that a sorted IDAM file organization would make an acceptable ISAM implementation. Even using a 35-bit descriptor we would expect fewer than six accesses on average to retrieve a record from a file of 1.44 million records.

We will defer further consideration of performance until the next chapter where suitable performance metrics are introduced. We will then be able to assess more fully the effects observed here.

5.7   Summary and Limitations

There are two principal reasons why the model of sorted D-trees expressed in recurrence (5.1) is only an approximation of the actual behavior.

1. The field behavior is not independent; that is, the probability of a transition in field j is influenced by the probability of a transition in fields $1, 2, \ldots, j - 1$.
2. The probability of matching an existing bit given that a transition has occurred is not generally uniform and is not independent of the transition probability.

Even though these estimates are not sharp, it is easy to see that for fixed parameters, a D-tree with sorted descriptors will have considerably better performance than if the file is randomly organized. This performance is not obtained without cost, however. The maintenance of the tree is made more complicated by the necessity of preserving order on insertion. If the file is relatively static, it may be better to add new records to the end of the file and then, periodically resort the file to improve performance.

The observation that the high order fields are quite sparse while the low order fields are becoming saturated, leads to an opportunity to decrease storage overhead somewhat. Since the low order fields are not providing much discrimination when r is large, by the optimal access strategy of theorem 4.2, the index will not be entered at the highest level for queries specifying only the low order fields. The fields might as well be deleted at least from the highest index level. Subsequent retrieval operations would ignore these fields during search operations until the first level containing them is encountered. If the deleted fields are the only fields specified in a query then it would be necessary to enter the D-tree at a lower level with a potential reduction in retrieval performance.

One final observation: since retrieval on the higher order fields will have the greatest performance, the best expected performance will be achieved when the file is sorted by fields in decreasing order of their probability of being specified in a query.

6

Comparative Evaluation of
Access Methods

In this chapter we will make use of the analytic results obtained for randomly organized and sorted IDAM files to compare these organizations with the traditional inverted file organization for multi-attribute retrieval. We have chosen inverted files as the vehicle for comparison for several reasons. First, it is a well known technique and has been extensively analyzed. Second, the more exotic techniques for multi-attribute retrieval have most often been compared in the literature with inverted files. Thus, inverted files have served as a baseline structure when reporting performance results.

When a file designer is faced with a choice from among several alternative file organizations, he will need some basis on which to make an intelligent selection. Often this is done by evaluating the candidates in light of the anticipated file characteristics. Two important performance measures influencing the choice are the *storage overhead* required to support the access method and the *expected retrieval performance* of the file organization. Other considerations may include the complexity of the method and implementation difficulty, but these factors are primarily of interest to the implementor not the user. Since we are interested in evaluating file organizations from the user's point of view, we will assume the software exists for each access method and concern ourselves only with issues related to performance.

In the next sections we will develop the concepts of storage overhead and retrieval performance more fully and introduce the specific performance metrics used in subsequent comparisons. The inverted file organization is described in enough detail to provide the information necessary for comparisons.

6.1 Storage Overhead

The storage overhead due to a retrieval mechanism may arise from several sources: (1) auxiliary index structures necessary to implement the retrieval mechanism; (2) pointers necessary in linked access methods; or (3) unused storage between records that are not tightly packed in the space allocated for the data file. These factors will all influence the total secondary storage requirement. There may also be additional primary storage requirements necessitated by stored tables or large code segments needed to implement complex methods. Although primary memory usage is typically more costly in computing environments, it will generally be moderate for most access methods. We will therefore confine our consideration of storage overhead to the secondary storage requirement of each file organization.

To measure the storage overhead due to an access method, the typical approach is to express the absolute overhead as a percentage of the data file size. That is,

$$\frac{size(\text{excess})}{size(\text{data file})}. \tag{6.1}$$

Note that we call the numerator "*size*(excess)" instead of "*size*(index)" as might seem more natural. Clearly, *size*(excess) will include the size of an index, but it will also include any increase in the storage of the data file which should properly be charged to the access method. Thus we will define

size(excess) = total storage required − *size*(data file).

Although this is certainly a measure of interest to the file designer in a specific application, we contend that from a theoretical viewpoint (6.1) does not accurately reflect the true overhead due to the access method. Consequently we propose a normalized measure of storage overhead.

Since the file organization supports retrieval on specific keys, it seems more appropriate to express the overhead as a function of the space required to store the keys. We may rewrite (6.1) as

$$\frac{size(\text{excess})}{size(\text{key part}) + size(\text{non-key part})}$$

where we have broken the data file into two parts. Since in general *size*(excess) is fixed regardless of the magnitude of *size*(non-key part), we propose the following measure of relative storage overhead:

$$SO = \frac{size(\text{excess})}{size(\text{key part})}. \tag{6.2}$$

This metric will more accurately reflect the inherent storage overhead of a file organization and will serve as a yardstick for the relative magnitude of the absolute overhead.

When comparing competing methods according to storage overhead we will often use the ratio

$$\frac{SO_i}{\min_k SO_k} \qquad (6.3)$$

for each method i. Note that when forming this ratio the choice of SO is irrelevant since (6.3) is equivalent to

$$\frac{size(\text{excess}_i)}{\min_k size(\text{excess}_k)} .$$

To minimize the number of assumptions about file characteristics necessary to calculate the storage overhead SO of (6.2), we will define a *minimal data file* to be a data file comprised only of key attributes where the size of the attribute values is minimal. That is, we assume a dense encoding of the domains, V_j, of the permissible values for each attribute. Thus, attribute j will require $\lceil \log | V_j | \rceil$ bits to store each value. Hence,

$$size(\text{key part}) = N \sum_{j=1}^{f} \lceil \log | V_j | \rceil . \qquad (6.4)$$

This may be an unrealistic estimate of the actual $size(\text{key part})$ of a typical data file, but it will give a worst case SO useful in rankings and will not affect the ratios (6.3) at all. Combining this estimate for $size(\text{key part})$ with equation (6.2) yields our normalized storage overhead metric,

$$SO = \frac{size(\text{excess})}{N \sum_{j=1}^{f} \lceil \log | V_j | \rceil} \qquad (6.5)$$

which can be used to evaluate a file organization once an expression for $size(\text{excess})$ is obtained.

6.2 Retrieval Performance

One of the most important criteria governing the choice of multi-attribute file organizations is the expected retrieval performance of the resultant system. This is also one of the most difficult aspects to assess in a general way. Ideally, one should express retrieval performance with respect to the set of anticipated queries. In fact, this is precisely what a file designer would do for his specific application. Since we will be dealing with hypothetical files and situations, a more general mechanism will be necessary. In this section we outline our approach to retrieval performance evaluation where the performance criterion is the expected number of secondary storage accesses.

In an actual retrieval environment it is possible to monitor query activity and gather statistics on the types of queries that users pose to the retrieval system. Specifically, one can determine an empirical query distribution specifying for each possible query the probability that the query will be posed to the system. We have no basis for assuming some particular query distribution *a priori*. Therefore we will consider instead the more general concept of *query patterns*.

A *query pattern*, *QP*, is an *f*-tuple, $QP = (x_1, x_2, \ldots, x_f)$, $x_j \in \{0,1\}$, where $x_j = 1$ if attribute a_j is specified in the query, and $x_j = 0$ if it is not. These query patterns have also been called partial-match patterns by Lin, Lee and Du (1979). For a file indexed on *f* fields, there are 2^f query patterns dividing all $\Pi \mid V_j \mid$ possible queries into classes. We will investigate the retrieval performance of multi-attribute file organizations with respect to query patterns.

In order to distinguish the classes of queries or query patterns from one another, we associate an integer *k* with each query pattern where *k* is formed by interpreting the pattern as a binary number. That is,

$$k = 2^{f-1}x_1 + 2^{f-2}x_2 + \ldots + 2^{f-j}x_j + \ldots + 2x_{f-1} + x_f.$$

We will denote each query pattern as QP_k. For example, QP_0 denotes the null query, while QP_{2^f-1} is the fully specified query.

It is important to note the distinction between actual queries and query patterns. This can be illustrated as follows. Suppose we have a file indexed on the three attributes NAME, AGE and SEX. Figure 6.1 shows all possible query patterns. The distinct queries

$$\{AGE = 18 \textbf{ AND } SEX = male\} \text{ and } \{AGE = 21 \textbf{ AND } SEX = female\}$$

are both members of the class QP_3.

We note that a file organization optimized with respect to query patterns may not be optimal with respect to individual queries. Lin, Lee and Du (1979) give an example of this phenomenon. However, we are not concerned with optimality issues here. We are concerned with the evaluation of file organizations and hence, will calculate expected retrieval performance as secondary storage accesses averaged over all query patterns.

The distribution of query patterns can be characterized as follows. Let p_j denote the probability that a_j, $1 \leq j \leq f$, occurs in a query. The probability that QP_k occurs, denoted qp_k, is given by

$$qp_k = \left(\prod_{x_j=1} p_j \right) \left(\prod_{x_j=0} (1-p_j) \right), \; x_j \in QP_k. \tag{6.6}$$

Here we have assumed that the fields are independently specified in a query.

Figure 6.1. Query Patterns

Class	Pattern	Attributes		
QP_0	(0,0,0)	----,	---,	---
QP_1	(0,0,1)	----,	---,	SEX
QP_2	(0,1,0)	----,	AGE,	---
QP_3	(0,1,1)	----,	AGE,	SEX
QP_4	(1,0,0)	NAME,	---,	---
QP_5	(1,0,1)	NAME,	---,	SEX
QP_6	(1,1,0)	NAME,	AGE,	---
QP_7	(1,1,1)	NAME,	AGE,	SEX

If we denote the expected number of secondary storage accesses required to satisfy a query of type QP_k by α_k, then the expected retrieval performance averaged over all possible query patterns, denoted by $E0$, is given by

$$E0 = \sum_{k=0}^{2^f-1} qp_k \alpha_k. \tag{6.7}$$

$E0$ can be used as one measure of retrieval performance. Unfortunately, due to the manner in which we have chosen to express the query pattern occurrence probabilities (6.6), the class QP_0 consisting of the null query will occur with nonzero probability. Specifically,

$$qp_0 = \prod_{j=1}^{f} (1 - p_j).$$

In practice we would not expect this query to be posed in an interactive environment. We will therefore evaluate file organizations with this query specifically removed from consideration and denote the adjusted performance metric by $E1$. Since

$$E0 = qp_0 \alpha_0 + (1 - qp_0)E1,$$

we have

$$E1 = \frac{E0 - qp_0 \alpha_0}{(1 - qp_0)} = \frac{\sum\limits_{k=1}^{2^f-1} qp_k \alpha_k}{(1 - qp_0)}. \tag{6.8}$$

One special distribution of query patterns results when each attribute is equally likely to occur in a pattern. This implies that $p_j = \frac{1}{2}$ for all f attributes. Then

$$qp_k = (\tfrac{1}{2})^q \, (\tfrac{1}{2})^{f-q} = \frac{1}{2^f};$$

that is, each query pattern is equally likely to occur. In this case

$$E0 = \frac{1}{2^f} \sum_{k=0}^{2^f-1} \alpha_k$$

and

$$E1 = \frac{1}{2^f - 1} \sum_{k=1}^{2^f-1} \alpha_k.$$

Although this distribution is unlikely in practice, it will serve as a useful baseline comparator.

As in the case of storage overhead, we will compare competing file organizations by means of the ratio

$$\frac{E1_i}{\min_k E1_k}.$$

6.3   Inverted Files

As mentioned at the outset of this chapter, the specific multi-attribute file organization we will be using in our comparisons is the inverted file structure. In this section we detail the specific model to be used in all subsequent comparisons. The *de facto* standard used in the literature for discussing inverted files is the model of Cardenas (1975). We will follow this model using essentially the approach of Liou and Yao (1977), with some appropriate simplifying assumptions.

In Cardenas' model an inverted file system is comprised of three parts: (1) a track index; (2) key-value index blocks; and (3) accession blocks. The key-value index blocks contain for each attribute-value pair a pointer to the accession list containing the addresses of the records having the specified value for the particular attribute. The accession lists are stored in the accession blocks. The track index is used to rapidly locate the appropriate key-value index blocks.

Cardenas gives detailed expressions for calculating the storage requirements of inverted files which we simplify as follows. The key-value index must contain one entry for each attribute-value pair comprised of the attribute, its value, and a pointer to the appropriate accession list. The size of an entry is therefore

$$size(\text{key-value entry}) = size(a_j) + size(v_j) + size(\text{pointer})$$

bits. Using the densest encoding and fixed field sizes, the sizes of the components can be represented by: (1) $size(a_j) = \log f$; (2) $size(v_j) = \log| V_j |$; and (3) $size(\text{pointer}) = \log N$. Since each attribute-value pair must be represented, there are

$$\sum_{j=1}^{f} | V_j |$$

entries. Therefore, the total size of the key-value index can be approximated by

$$size(\text{key-value index}) = \sum_{j=1}^{f} | V_j | \left(\log | V_j | + \log N\right) \qquad (6.9)$$

bits. Here we have neglected the small contribution of $size(a_j)$.

The track index will contain one entry for each page in the key-value index and hence, will have size

$$size(\text{track index}) = \frac{size(\text{key-value index})}{(\# \text{ bits per page})} \; size(\text{key-value entry}). \qquad (6.10)$$

Since each record address must appear on f accession lists the size of the accession lists will be approximately

$$size(\text{accession lists}) = fN \log N,$$

which is in general the dominant component of the storage requirement. Combining with equations (6.9) and (6.10) and simplifying yields for the storage requirement of an inverted file

$$size(\text{inverted file}) = Z \sum_{j=1}^{f} | V_j | \left(\log | V_j | + \log N\right) + fN \log N \qquad (6.11)$$

where Z is given by

$$Z = 1 + \frac{size(\text{key-value entry})}{(\# \text{ bits per page})}.$$

This is the expression we will use throughout for calculating the storage requirement of inverted files.

Turning now to the retrieval performance of inverted files, we will assume that each query can be satisfied with one access to the track index. Each attribute specified will require one access to the key-value index to locate the appropriate accession list and one access per block to fetch the accession list. Thus, a query on q attributes will require

$$1 + q + \sum_{j \in Q} B_j$$

access in the index, where B_j denotes the number of blocks in the jth accession list. Often the accession lists will be short and reside in one block each. In this case, the number of accesses in the index is simply $1 + 2q$.

Since our performance measure counts only the expected number of accesses to satisfy a query, we will ignore the cost of intersecting the accession lists and will only be interested in the expected size of the resultant list. This corresponds to the expected number of data records satisfying the query. Under the usual assumption that the attribute values are equally likely, we would expect

$$\bar{R} = \frac{N}{\prod_{j \in Q} |V_j|} \qquad (6.12)$$

records to satisfy the query and moreover, these $\bar{R}$ records may be considered to be randomly distributed among the blocks of the data file.

This assumption of random distribution of the $\bar{R}$ records manifestly increases the expected number of block accesses in comparison to any clustered organization. In the worst case, $\bar{R}$ blocks will have to be accessed reflecting the possibility that each record is in a different block. In general, however, we would expect fewer blocks to be accessed on average. Cardenas and others have used the following approximation for block accesses:

$$B \left[1 - \left(1 - \frac{1}{B}\right)^{\bar{R}} \right] \qquad (6.13)$$

where B denotes the number of data blocks in the file and R is given by equation (6.12).

Yao (1977) has given an exact expression for the expected number of block accesses, but has shown that for blocking factors of 10 or greater, the error in the approximation (6.13) is practically negligible. Consequently in order to remain consistent with other reported performance results, we too will use (6.13) to estimate data block accesses.

In summary, the expected number of block accesses necessary to satisfy a query on q attributes in an inverted file system can be estimated by the expression

$$1 + q + \sum_{j \in Q} B_j + B \left[1 - \left(1 - \frac{1}{B}\right)^{\bar{R}} \right] \qquad (6.14)$$

where B_j is the number of blocks in accession list j, $\bar{R}$ is given by equation (6.12), and B denotes the number of data blocks in the file.

6.4 Performance Comparisons

In this section we will investigate further the behavior of the sorted IDAM files described in chapter 5. This will include comparisons with inverted files. We will begin by considering the example of section 5.4 in more detail. The parameters used in the example are summarized in table 6.1.

We have observed that there are two ways in which the performance of sorted IDAM files can be influenced: (1) the widths of the low order fields can be increased; or (2) the size of the bucket space can be decreased. Case A in table 6.1 represents a large (1,440,000 records) IDAM file reported in the literature (Pfaltz, Berman and Cagley 1980). For this file, we have already seen (see tables 5.3 and 5.4) that the low order fields are providing little if any discrimination to the search procedure. Cases B and C attempt to improve this situation by increasing the low order field widths. In case D the size of the bucket space has been reduced.

The size of a fully packed D-tree as given by equation (3.11) is

$$wN \sum_{i=1}^{h} \frac{1}{r_i} \text{ where } r_i = \prod_{k=0}^{i-1} b_k. \tag{6.15}$$

Recall that r_i is the number of data records covered by a descriptor at level i. In this example, $r_1 = 24$ and $r_2 = 3072$.

Using the data in table 6.1 and the expressions in (6.15), the storage overhead for each of the cases A–D can be computed. These values are shown in table 6.2. The quantity SO is the normalized storage overhead metric of equation (6.5). It is just the size of the index over the minimum data file size. The increased field widths of cases B and C are reflected in SO while case D decreased by 50 percent as expected.

Table 6.1. Data Used in Example of Section 5.4

Case	Descriptor Format
A	(10,10,10,10,10,10,10)
B	(10,10,10,10,50,50,50)
C	(10,10,10,10,100,100,100)
D	(5,5,5,5,5,5,5)

Number of records	1,440,000
Total descriptors	60,469
Blocking factors	
Data	24
Index	128
Minimum Data File	40,320 Kb

Table 6.2. Storage Overhead

	A	B	C	D
Width	70	190	340	35
Overhead (Kb)	4232.83	11489.11	20559.46	2116.42
SO	.11	.29	.51	.05

Table 6.3. Retrieval Performance

Number Attributes	Number Queries	Expected Accesses			
		A	B	C	D
1	7	22568.5	11963.8	8709.8	14951.0
2	21	7063.6	2298.0	1338.1	3669.6
3	35	1791.0	460.0	257.3	908.2
4	35	399.7	107.1	70.5	230.7
5	21	85.1	29.5	23.5	61.2
6	7	18.4	8.8	7.9	17.4
7	1	4.5	3.0	2.9	5.6
	$E1$	3030.8	1201.1	796.0	1755.8

Table 6.4. Performance Comparison

	A	B	C	D
SO / SO_A	1.00	2.71	4.86	.50
$E1 / E1_A$	1.00	.40	.26	.58

The expected number of block accesses given a query Q can be calculated from equation (4.6) and is

$$\bar{a}(Q) = \bar{a}_h + \sum_{i=1}^{h} N_i \prod_{j \in Q} \frac{\bar{s}_j(r)}{w_j}. \qquad (6.16)$$

To get the most conservative estimate, we will use the upper bound of corollary 5.4.1 as the estimate of $\bar{s}_j(r)$. These calculations are shown in table 6.3. Assuming that every query pattern is equally likely, the weighted performance metric $E1$ (see equation 6.8) is given by

$$E1 = \frac{1}{2^f - 1} \sum_{k=1}^{2^f-1} \alpha_k$$

where α_k is computed for each query class k by equation (6.16).

Note from table 6.3 that both strategies (i.e., increasing field widths or reducing the size of the bucket space) result in improved retrieval performance. The increased sensitivity gained by doubling the field widths from 50 to 100 in case C is most marked when few attributes are specified. Although the strategy of reducing the size of the bucket space (case D) results in an improvement over case A, the improvement is less pronounced than in cases B and C.

To assess the cost of the performance gains in cases B–D, the storage overhead SO and the weighted number of accesses $E1$ have been normalized against case A. These are shown in table 6.4. It can be seen that case C achieves the greatest performance gain, but at the greatest cost. This is the classic space/time tradeoff. Although cases B–D all improve the performance of the system, only case D actually lowers the storage overhead. Here an improvement has been attained in both performance and storage overhead.

Because the situation in this example (i.e., small attribute domain sizes) is so unfavorable to inverted files, we will consider a more balanced example for comparison. In this example we will consider three files ranging from small to very large. The files consist of $N = 3,000,000$, $N = 50,000$, and $N = 1,000$ records, respectively. The other file characteristics are summarized in table 6.5 and are the same for each size.

For this example, we will assume that a record is indexed on 14 fields. For simplicity we will assume only two domain sizes. Seven of the fields have 20 values in their domains. These fields would correspond to such information as department numbers, marital status or other coded information. The remaining fields are assumed to have 1000 values in their underlying domains. These fields would correspond, for example, to numeric information.

We will assume a common page size of 512 bytes and let all data files be blocked five records per block. This is reasonable, since we would like to have fully packed pages or nearly so, and it is unlikely that a record of fewer than 100 bytes is of practical use.

Table 6.5.   Comparison Parameters

Number of attributes	14

Domain sizes	
(1–7)	20
(8–14)	1000

Page size (bytes)	512

Descriptor format	
(1–7)	4
(8–14)	16

Blocking factors	
Data (both)	5
Index (IDAM)	25

Table 6.6.   Storage Overhead

		Inverted File		IDAM	
N	Minimum Data File	Absolute	*SO*	Absolute	*SO*
3,000,000	315,000	924,230	2.93	87,360	.28
50,000	5250	11,386	2.17	1,456	.28
1,000	105	283	2.69	29	.28

The IDAM files have descriptors with 4-bit fields corresponding to the domains with 20 values and 16-bit fields for the 1000 value domains. Thus, a descriptor has width $w = 140$ bits. These descriptors are assumed to be packed 25 per index block (page).

The storage overhead resulting from each method is shown in table 6.6 for each of the three file sizes considered. Again, the values for the IDAM files are calculated from (6.15). The inverted file storage overhead is determined by equation (6.11).

The quantity *SO* for the IDAM method is the same for all three file sizes. This is because none of the parameters have changed and the overhead is directly proportional to the number of data records. The variance in *SO* for the inverted

Table 6.7.   Retrieval Performance

Expected Accesses

Number Attributes	Number Queries	N = 3,000,000		N = 50,000		N = 1,000	
		Inverted File	IDAM	Inverted File	IDAM	Inverted File	IDAM
1	14	68269.6	165367.4	1138.5	3299.9	25.7	90.0
2	91	2627.4	46671.7	44.0	1133.8	5.6	40.4
3	364	1277.6	14733.7	21.2	453.9	7.0	20.0
4	1001	1651.8	5412.7	27.0	223.6	9.0	11.5
5	2002	2063.5	2299.9	33.5	132.7	11.0	8.0
6	3003	2476.0	1076.2	40.0	87.8	13.0	6.4
7	3432	2888.5	525.5	46.5	60.7	15.0	5.6
8	3003	3301.0	258.2	53.0	42.3	17.0	5.1
9	2002	3713.5	125.4	59.5	29.2	19.0	4.7
10	1001	4126.0	59.8	66.0	19.8	21.0	4.3
11	364	4538.5	28.0	72.5	13.2	23.0	4.0
12	91	4951.0	13.1	79.0	8.6	25.0	3.6
13	14	5363.5	6.3	85.5	5.6	27.0	3.3
14	1	5776.0	3.2	92.0	3.7	29.0	3.0
	E 1	2957.6	1714.0	47.7	90.8	15.0	6.7

files results principally from the different pointer sizes used for each file. In order to be most favorable to inverted files, the size of a pointer was chosen to be log N bits rather than being fixed at say 16 or 32 bits.

It is clear from table 6.6 that inverted files are more profligate in their use of storage than are IDAM files. For each file size, the inverted files are using approximately 10 times the space required by IDAM files. This was not unexpected. Wiederhold (1977) notes that when many attributes are inverted, the size of an inverted file will often exceed the size of the data file. One reason for this example is to show that with IDAM methods many attributes can be indexed with a reasonable storage cost.

The expected retrieval performance is shown in table 6.7. The values for the IDAM files are computed from equation (6.16) while those for the inverted files come from equation (6.14). Again, we have assumed that all query patterns are equally likely.

One characteristic of inverted files is evident from the data. Inverted files are most efficient when a small number of attributes are specified. Their performance is steadily degraded when more attributes are specified by the need to fetch more and more accession lists whatever their size. In contrast, the performance of IDAM files improves as more attributes are specified.

The IDAM files are superior to inverted files for the cases $N = 3,000,000$ and $N = 1,000$. In the former case, the inverted file is being degraded by long accession lists. In the latter, the number of accession lists fetched becomes dominant. The superiority of the inverted file for the case $N = 50,000$ results from its lower average number of accesses on queries of 4 to 10 attributes where approximately 94% of the queries occur in this distribution. The storage cost of this structure (see table 6.6) is, however, excessive.

In the next chapter we consider alternate ways to improve the performance of IDAM files.

7

Top-down Methods for IDAM Files

Thus far we have only considered IDAM organizations in which the index is built on top of the data file, that is, the index file organization is an artifact of the data file organization. The retrieval performance of the IDAM files resulting from this bottom-up approach has been examined and the effects of changes in system parameters isolated. The primary factor governing retrieval performance is the relative saturation of the descriptors in the index. Unfortunately, the means available to control this saturation has not been entirely satisfying.

The analysis of randomly organized IDAM files led to the conclusion that if the number of records covered by a descriptor is large, the field widths in the descriptor will have to be made large to avoid saturation. Sorted IDAM file organizations are a bit more flexible with regard to fine tuning, but still rely ultimately on the adjustment of field widths to control saturation and alter retrieval performance. It does not seem entirely natural to be forced to change the widths of fields to improve retrieval performance. In many applications there may be other reasons for choosing field widths and once chosen these widths should remain fixed. For this reason, we want to consider alternate organizations that provide good retrieval performance, but also allow a greater freedom in the choice of these parameters. In this chapter we will consider some top-down IDAM file organizations that offer promise in this area.

7.1 Top-down Organizations

As we indicated earlier, the distinction between bottom-up methods and top-down methods is whether the index is consulted during record insertion to determine a location for the data record. Bottom-up methods first add the record to the data file and then update the index accordingly. Top-down methods make use of the index in an effort to cluster the data records according to some criterion. In this way it is hoped that an improvement in retrieval performance will be realized.

It should be noted at the outset of this discussion that top-down organizations are completely determined by a prespecified *insertion* algorithm. The retrieval algorithm *DFS* outlined in figure 3.3 will work correctly with any IDAM organization. It is the insertion algorithm that will determine the shape of the resulting tree and hence, the storage overhead required to store the tree and the cost to search it.

The bottom-up insertion algorithm implicitly assumed for the construction of the randomly organized and sorted IDAM files of chapters 4 and 5 is outlined below. We will call this simple insertion procedure algorithm *BU*.

Assume that a record *R* with descriptor *D(R)* is to be inserted into the data file.

Algorithm *BU*:

    1. If the last block in the data level is not full, add *R* to that block. Otherwise, create a new data block at the end of the data file with *R* as its only record.

    2. Update the index accordingly.

Clearly many details have been buried in step 2. In addition to updating the descriptors along the record access path, updating the index may require the creation of new index blocks at different levels as well as the maintenance of global data about the file. Since these factors are essentially coding details, we will not consider them further.

It is easy to see that algorithm *BU* will always create a full tree with no unused space except that resulting from the potentially incomplete packing of the last block at each level. Algorithm *BU* therefore builds the best trees from a storage viewpoint. As we have noted, the performance of this organization is determined by the placement of the data records, that is, the order of the records during insertion.

Several heuristic insertion algorithms and strategies are possible. We will briefly and informally summarize some of these heuristics and consider the most promising approach in greater detail.

The conceptual vehicle used to model top-down insertion procedures is a bounded breadth first search (BBFS) of the index to locate the "best" data block in which to place a given record. The BBFS is constrained to retain only the m_i most promising blocks at level i. The parameters m_i are selectable and typically are different for different heuristics. The determination of which blocks to save is based on a set of cost functions that completely specify the nature of the insertion heuristic. These cost functions assign a figure of merit to each candidate block considered by the search process and thus serve to rank the candidates in order of preference. When two candidates evaluate to the same figure of merit a tie-breaking rule, the *early selection criterion*, is applied. This rule states that when two candidates are equally suitable, the one which would be encountered first by the retrieval process is to be preferred. This BBFS based insertion algorithm is quite general and can be varied from "greedy" to "exhaustive" by the specification of appropriate cost functions.

It will be helpful when discussing heuristic insertion algorithms to consider the algorithms as operating on nonempty files. The issue of file behavior when starting with an empty file is treated separately. We take this approach because the heuristics are better understood if we initially neglect the boundary condition.

In general, the principal objective of top-down organizations is to keep the number of bits set in a descriptor as low as possible. The first algorithm examined attempts to accomplish this goal in a straightforward manner. The heuristic rule is to place a data record in a block such that the weight increase in the descriptors along the access path is minimal. This heuristic is called *MW* for minimum weight increase. The operation is as follows.

Algorithm *MW*:

1. Search the highest level index saving those blocks, *B*, such that

$$weight(D(B) \lor D(R)) - weight(D(B)) \qquad (7.1)$$

is smallest.
2. For each block, *B*, saved in step 1, search all immediate successors at the next level evaluating them according to criterion (7.1).
3. Repeat this process until either: (a) a suitable data block is located—insert *R* into this block; or (b) no data block is found suitable—create a new data block.
4. Update the index accordingly.

A number of housekeeping details have been suppressed in this description. However, it is detailed enough to describe the operation of algorithm *MW*. If we imagine that the file exists and a new record is to be inserted, algorithm *MW* will place the record in that data block in which the fewest additional bits are set in the new block descriptor. Thus, the record is placed into that data block with which it has most in common, that is, is most similar to the records already there. Hence, algorithm *MW* exhibits a clustering property. It does, however, have a serious flaw.

Observation 7.1: If algorithm *MW* is used to build a file starting from an initially empty state, it will build the same tree as algorithm *BU*.

This occurs because the weight increase when adding a new block is equal to *f*, the number of fields in a descriptor. Since the weight increase in a partially filled block will be at most *f*, by the early selection criterion the partially filled block will be preferred.

Observation 7.1 would seem to negate the utility of algorithm *MW*. It can, however, be employed in an insertion strategy which uses some other technique to build an initial tree with partially packed data blocks. Algorithm *MW* can then be used to maintain the tree and reduce the rate of descriptor saturation. For example, a file of N records could be filled to one half its capacity using algorithm *BU*. The remaining $N/2$ records could then be inserted into the file using algorithm *MW*. Simulations have shown that this strategy will retain essentially the same retrieval performance while only slightly increasing the storage overhead. As will be seen, algorithm *MW* can also be used with a prespecified threshold to determine when "best" is "good enough."

Another heuristic approach is based on the observation that the retrieval process is a depth first search. It seems reasonable to insert a record in the first place that the search will look for it. In this way the insertion algorithm will parallel the retrieval process. We call this heuristic *FM* for first match. It operates as follows.

Algorithm *FM*:

1. Perform a retrieval for R using $D(R)$ as the query descriptor.
2. If a data block is matched, put R in that block. Otherwise, create a new block at the end of the file and insert R there.
3. Update the index accordingly.

This heuristic has a very intuitive appeal and can be expected to build trees which are optimized for retrieval, at least for fully qualified queries. However, this performance is purchased at considerable cost.

Observation 7.2: If algorithm *FM* is used to build a file starting from an initially empty state, it will build the worst possible tree from a storage overhead viewpoint.

Note that since algorithm *FM* requires an exact match for insertion, when it does not find a suitable data block it will not only create a new block, but also a new path from the root to the data level. If there are d distinct descriptors in a file of N records, the resulting tree will have d leaves containing approximately N/d records each and d paths from the root to the data level. (Theorem 5.2 can be used to calculate the expected number of distinct descriptors in a file given the descriptor format and the number of data records.)

Thus, when starting with an initially empty file, algorithm *FM* partitions the file by descriptor but does not perform any further clustering. Again like algorithm *MW*, algorithm *FM* could be used in a hybrid insertion strategy that seeks to maintain some performance level.

Algorithm *MW* can be generalized to encompass a class of insertion heuristics by introducing a threshold requirement to criterion (7.1). That is,

$$weight\big(D(B) \vee D(R)\big) - weight(D(B)) \leqslant k \qquad (7.2)$$

where $0 \leqslant k \leqslant f$. Call this heuristic $MW(k)$. Indeed, it is possible to generalize further by specifying a different constant k_i for each level i.

Observation 7.3: Algorithm *FM* is equivalent to *MW*(0) and algorithm *MW* is equivalent to $MW(f)$.

Thus, algorithm $MW(k)$ can be varied from algorithm *BU* (see observation 7.1) at one extreme to algorithm *FM* at the other. This means that algorithm $MW(k)$ can be made to produce trees at each extreme as well, from best to worst. Simulations have shown that the resulting trees are exceedingly sparse and involve much wasted space, particularly when small files are used.

    These approaches are not particularly promising due to the low level of clustering achieved and the large storage overhead associated with the indexes constructed. They also have undesirable behavior when given an initially empty file. In the next section we discuss a clustering procedure which overcomes many of the problems discussed here.

7.2 Convex Clustering

The primary deficiency of the heuristic approaches described so far is their inability to create files with good performance when starting from an initially empty state. They are best used in a hybrid strategy where some preprocessing has been done on the data file to form *clusters* of items. By a cluster we mean a group of data records judged to be similar under some criterion. In this context, the heuristic approaches of the last section can be useful as a means of maintaining the clusters. It is far more desirable to have a method that is able to cluster data on the fly during record insertion and thus work satisfactorily beginning with an empty file. One such technique, called *convex clustering*, has been described by Pfaltz (1982). This method is concerned with the creation of convex clusters formed by the random placement of items in a discrete *m*-dimensional space and was developed to facilitate range searching as well as partial match retrieval.

    In this method data records are grouped into dynamically formed convex clusters as they are inserted into a file. A cluster is said to be *convex* if and only if it is a $b_1 \times b_2 \times \ldots \times b_m$-cube. As an example consider the sets of points depicted in figure 7.1. The sets $S1$ and $S3$ are convex, while $S2$ and $S4$ are not.

Figure 7.1. Sets in 2-dimensional Space

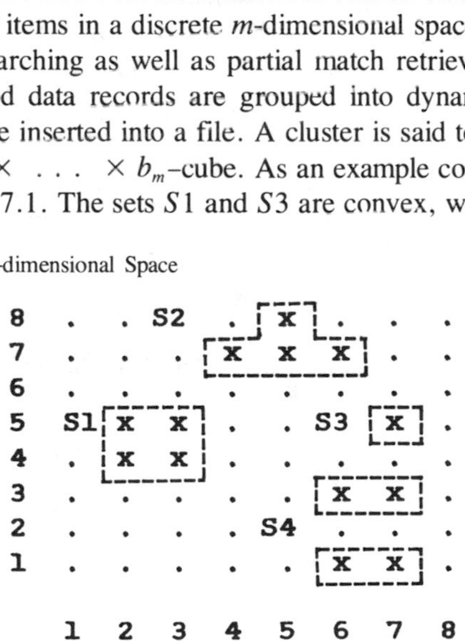

The descriptor for a convex set of points has the property that each field has b_j contiguous bits set. Thus for example, $D(S1) = 01100000\ 00011000$, while $D(S4) = 00000110\ 10100000$.

Pfaltz's algorithm (denoted by CC) proceeds as follows. Assume that a record R with descriptor $D(R)$ is to be inserted into the file.

Algorithm CC:

1. For each cluster C with descriptor $D(C)$, R can be added to C if and only if

$$D(R) \vee D(C) \text{ is convex.} \qquad (7.3)$$

2. If only one cluster satisfies (7.3) then R is added to that cluster. If two or more clusters satisfy (7.3), R is added to the cluster containing the fewest records.
3. If no cluster satisfies (7.3), a new cluster is started.

The new cluster $C' = C \cup \{R\}$ and has descriptor $D(C') = D(R) \vee D(C)$. Note that the set of points defined by the records in a cluster is not necessarily convex, but the cluster is. This is because the cluster may contain points to which no records have been mapped. The cluster represented by $D(C)$ is in fact the *convex hull* of the points defined by the records.

Pfaltz defines two volume measures regarding these clusters: *extent* and *content*. The extent of a cluster is the number of points contained in the cluster while the content is the number of records in it. The addition of a new record into an existing cluster will always increase the content by one, but may or may not increase the extent. The reader is referred to Pfaltz (1982) for further details.

The operation of the technique of convex clustering is most easily demonstrated by means of an example. For this example, we assume a two-dimensional space into which records are to be mapped. The descriptor format is (8,8) and the records to be considered along with the points to which they map are shown in table 7.1.

Consider the points *a, b, c,* and *d* entered into an initially empty file in the order given. A single cluster with extent $= 12$ and content $= 4$ will result. This

Table 7.1.   Data Records Used in Example

a	(2,3)
b	(3,4)
c	(4,5)
d	(5,4)
e	(3,5)
f	(3,5)

is shown in figure 7.2(a). Now suppose the same four records are entered in the order *a, b, d* and *c*. From algorithm *CC* it can be seen that two clusters, each with extent = 4 and content = 2, will be formed. This is shown in figure 7.2(b). Thus, the order in which records are inserted will affect the clustering of the file.

Continuing the example, suppose now that record *e* is inserted into the file depicted in figure 7.2(b). The result is shown in figure 7.2(c). If the point *f* is now inserted into the file, the clusters in figure 7.2(d) result. Note first that this situation is entirely possible since records need not uniquely map to points. Two observations may be made from figure 7.2(d). First, two records may be entered into the some point in the space, but they need not belong to the same cluster. From the figure it can be seen that {*a,b,e*} and {*c,d,f,*} are in different clusters (*C*1 and *C*2 respectively) yet *e* and *f* map to a point in the intersection of the clusters. From a retrieval standpoint, it would be more desirable to have *e* and *f* belong to the same cluster.

The second observation is that due to the increase in the extent of *C*2, the record *b* now lies in the intersection of *C*1 and *C*2. This means that any retrieval requesting record *b* will require the examination of *C*1 as well as *C*2.

Figure 7.2.   Example of the Operation of Algorithm *CC*

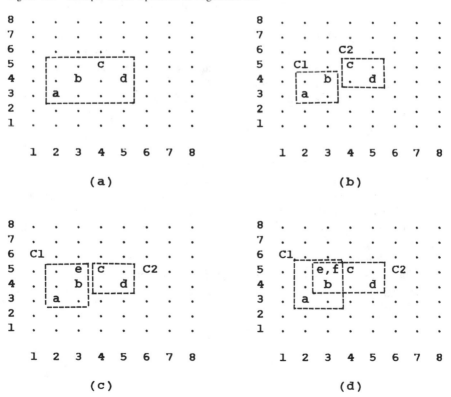

(a)

(b)

(c)

(d)

Pfaltz reported that the analysis of algorithm *CC* revealed that an equilibrium condition is eventually reached in which there is an upper bound on the number of partially filled blocks in the system. This phenomenon was also observed in the behavior of a simulator for the system. He also showed that storage overhead, as a percent of the total data file, decreases as *N*, the number of data records in the file, becomes large.

Although Pfaltz shows that algorithm *CC* has good retrieval performance, there are some drawbacks. As we have noted, the clustering mechanism is dependent on the order in which the records are inserted. It is therefore possible to build files with widely differing retrieval performance over the same data set merely by permuting the data records. It is not clear what ordering will result in the best performance. Indeed, it is likely that if the data file is sorted and the content of clusters is bounded, the structure and performance of files constructed by algorithm *CC* will be similar to the sorted files described in chapter 5.

We have also noted that algorithm *CC* allows clusters to overlap. The effects of this phenomenon are not clearly understood. It seems clear, though, that retrieval performance is likely to be adversely affected by the need to examine all clusters having a common intersection when retrieving a record in that intersection.

The most serious drawback to algorithm *CC* is that it only constructs a single level index which may encompass a very large number of clusters. It is not clear how one would aggregate the level 1 clusters into higher levels. Hence, because algorithm *CC* requires an exhaustive search of all the clusters, a single level index could seriously impair its efficiency. Note here that the problem is not the fact that algorithm *CC* requires an exhaustive search for insertion, rather it is the cost of that search which may be prohibitive.

To overcome the disadvantages of algorithm *CC* while retaining the desirable properties, we consider a variant heuristic called *disjoint convex clustering (DDC)*. In this method the space is considered to be prepartitioned into regions. Records are inserted into clusters residing in these regions based on their location within the space and irrespective of the order of insertion.

The conceptual partitioning of the space by this method is hierarchical. That is, at the highest level the space is partioned coarsely. Subsequent levels increasingly refine the partitioning by breaking large regions into smaller disjoint regions. This has the effect of increasing the resolution of a search as it proceeds through the index.

Algorithm *DCC* can be stated quite simply. Again assume that a record *R* with descriptor $D(R)$ is to be inserted into the file. Let *C* denote an arbitrary cluster and let $region_i(x)$ denote the region of the space containing the entity *x* under the level *i* partitioning. The operation of algorithm *DCC* is as follows.

Algorithm *DCC*:

    1.   Set *i* to the highest index level.

2. If there exists a cluster C at level i such that $region_i(R) = region_i(C)$, insert the record R into C. That is,

$$C = C \cup \{R\} \text{ and } D(C) = D(C) \vee D(R).$$

3. If no such C exists, create a new cluster $C = \{R\}$ where $D(C) = D(R)$.
4. Repeat steps 2 and 3 for all index levels.

As an example of the operation of algorithm *DCC*, again consider the file of figure 7.2(d). In this example, we assume that at level 2 the space is partitioned into 4×4 regions. The level 2 regions are further subdivided at level 1 into 2×2 regions. The allocation of the records $\{a,b,c,d,e,f\}$ to clusters by algorithm *DCC* is shown in figure 7.3.

Algorithm *DCC* constructs a multi-level index so the main objection to algorithm *CC* has been overcome. Notice from the figure that the records $\{e,f\}$ now reside in the same cluster. In addition, a retrieval requesting record b now need only look at one cluster per level. In fact any fully qualified retrieval can be satisfied by examining precisely one cluster per level. This follows from the fact that the clusters are disjoint. It should be noted, however, that accessing one cluster may necessitate several block accesses depending on the method used to store a cluster and its overall size.

The fact that the clusters are disjoint also means that insertion will be efficient. Since insertion is the analog of a fully qualified retrieval, at most one cluster per index level will be accessed during insertion.

Figure 7.3. Disjoint Convex Clusters

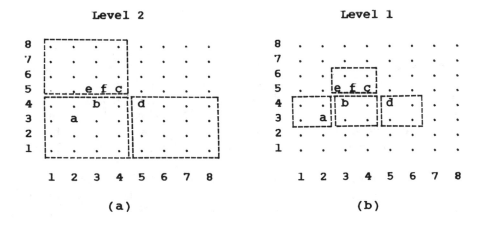

7.3   Retrieval Performance of Algorithm *DCC*

The idea of partitioning a multi-dimensional data space is not new and has been discussed by many authors (see for example, Bentley (1975), Berman and Pfaltz (1978), Finkel and Bentley (1974), Lee and Wong (1980), Lin, Lee and Du (1979), and Liou and Yao (1977)) in connection with a variety of retrieval systems. In the most related work, Liou and Yao described a retrieval method called the *multi-dimensional directory* (MDD). In this method each attribute domain V_i is partitioned into m_i approximately equal sized intervals ($| V_i |/m_i$). Records are placed in buckets corresponding to the resultant subregions and a directory of these subregions is maintained. It is easy to see that the specification of q attributes in a query will reduce the number of buckets examined by a factor of $\Pi_i m_i$ where i indexes the q attributes specified. In fact, algorithm *DCC* is very similar to the MDD, the principal difference being in the structure of the index or directory.

In another related work, Aho and Ullman (1979) discuss the optimal assignment of bits to fields when the fields are independently specified in queries. Although their work concerned hashing schemes, it can be applied to the selection of field widths for IDAM file structures. The interested reader is referred to their paper for further details. In the discussion to follow, we will assume that the field widths for a descriptor (i.e., the descriptor format) have already been chosen.

To assess the retrieval performance of algorithm *DCC*, it is necessary to examine the structure of the descriptors appearing in each level of the index. The simple two-dimensional example of figure 7.3 will be used throughout this discussion for illustrative purposes.

Suppose we have an *f*-dimensional space defined by the descriptor format $(w_1, w_2, \ldots, w_f)$. Although the partition specified at each level can be quite general, we will assume for simplicity that each field j in a descriptor at level i is divided into m_{ij} equal pieces. Let

$$b_{ij} = \frac{w_j}{m_{ij}}$$

denote the maximum number of bits that can be set in field j of a descriptor at level i. Note that b_{ij} denotes an interval or range of values along the jth dimension.

Let m_i denote the number of regions the space is partitioned into at level i. Using this notation it can be seen that at level i the space will be partitioned into $b_{i1} \times b_{i2} \times \ldots \times b_{if}$–cubes and there will be $m_i = \prod_{j=1}^{f} m_{ij}$ such cubes. In the example of figure 7.3 where $w_1 = w_2 = 8$, there are $m_2 = 4$ (4 × 4)–cubes at level 2 and $m_1 = 16$ (2 × 2)–cubes at level 1, since $m_{21} = m_{22} = 2$ and $m_{11} = m_{12} = 4$.

The performance of files constructed by algorithm *DCC* will depend on the relationship between the extent of clusters and the volume of the regions in which they are formed (their defining regions). To illustrate the difference in these terms, consider the set of points $\{c,e,f\}$ in figure 7.3. This set of points lies in a cluster with extent $= 2$ and content $= 3$. The volume of the defining region is 4.

Since we have assumed that all regions at a given level are the same size, the volume of a region at level i is just the total number of points in the space divided by the number of regions in the partition at level i. Recall that the total volume of the space is $v_f = \prod_{j=1}^{f} w_j$, so that the number of points in a region is

$$\frac{v_f}{m_i} = \prod_{j=1}^{f} b_{ij} \tag{7.4}$$

as expected. Expression (7.4) is also the maximum extent of a cluster at level i. The extent of a cluster can encompass the entire volume of its defining region when the number of records in the cluster (i.e., its content) is as few as $\max_{j=1}^{f} b_{ij}$ records. This will occur when by chance the points to which the records map lie diagonally across the region.

Consider any field j in a descriptor at level i. Under the level i partition, there will be at most b_{ij} contiguous bits set in the descriptor. We can determine the expected number of bits set in the descriptor as a function of the cluster content as follows.

Suppose that a new record is to be added to a cluster by algorithm *DCC*. The fact that the new record is to be entered into the cluster means that the bit set in field j of the record descriptor must be one of the b_{ij} bits in the jth interval of the cluster. Since the new bit is equally likely to match an existing bit, the probability of this event is $1/b_{ij}$. Alternatively, the new bit will not match an existing bit (that is, a transition will occur) with probability

$$1 - \frac{1}{b_{ij}} .$$

Recall that the conditions of the model of theorem 5.5 are

1. The probability of a transition occurring and the probability of matching an existing bit are independent, and
2. The new bit is equally likely to match an existing bit.

In the case that we are examining, these conditions clearly hold. Therefore, the model of theorem 5.5 can be applied. Hence, by corollary 5.5.1(b), the expected number of bits set in field j of the descriptor is

$$\bar{s}_j(r) = b_{ij} \left[1 - \left(1 - \frac{1}{b_{ij}} \right)^r \right] \tag{7.5}$$

It is clear from equation (7.5) that the subfields saturate at a rapid rate. This is not an unexpected result given the way in which the descriptors are constructed.

To estimate when this saturation is likely to occur, we approximate equation (7.5) by

$$\bar{s}(r) \approx b \left(1 - e^{-r/b}\right) \tag{7.6}$$

(see section 4.3). Here we have dropped the subscripts to simplify the notation.

A conservative estimate of when to expect saturation can be obtained by determining when $\bar{s}(r) = b - 1$. From equation (7.6) this will occur approximately when $b \left(1 - e^{-r/b}\right) = b - 1$, from which it follows that $r = b \ln b$. We conclude from this expression that the field will have all b_{ij} bits set with high probability when

$$r \geqslant b_{ij} \ln b_{ij}. \tag{7.7}$$

Although (7.7) gives an estimate of when to expect all b_{ij} bits to be set in any particular field, it does not follow that all the fields in a descriptor will simultaneously have all b_{ij} bits set. However, since in most situations the quantity $b \ln b$ is small, it is reasonable to expect all the fields to have their b_{ij} bits set, particularly when r/b_{ij} is very large. Hence, (7.7) can be used in all practical situations as a yardstick for estimating when a cluster can be expected to cover its defining region.

The fact that clusters, at least in the higher index levels, will rapidly expand to encompass the volume of their defining regions is not surprising. Since the partitioning of the space at the higher index levels is very coarse and records are uniformly distributed throughout it, one may expect a relatively few records to span the space. As we will see this phenomenon does not unduly degrade performance and leads to an opportunity to decrease the storage overhead of the index markedly while retaining the same level of retrieval performance. This will be discussed further at the end of this section.

The probability of matching any field j in a descriptor at level i will be no worse than b_{ij}/w_j. The safest course when evaluating the performance of algorithm *DCC* is therefore to assume that

$$\rho_{ij} = \frac{b_{ij}}{w_j}. \tag{7.8}$$

To get some feel for the behavior of files constructed by algorithm *DCC*, we return to the example of chapter 6. Recall that the data file being examined contained 1,440,000 records. To apply algorithm *DCC* in a manner comparable to the sorted technique used in the example, we chose a descriptor format of seven 8-bit fields. This leads to a space of $v_f = 8^7$ points. The fields were partitioned into $m_{1j} = 4$ and $m_{2j} = 2$ pieces at levels 1 and 2, respectively. Thus, there are $m_1 = 4^7 = 16,384$ regions in the level 1 index and $m_2 = 2^7 = 128$ regions in the level 2 index. Each level 2 region covers 128 level 1 regions.

The relevant parameters from the example of chapter 6 are summarized in table 7.2. Cases A through D are the files constructed by algorithm *BU* from initially sorted data files. Case E represents the file constructed by algorithm *DCC*.

Table 7.2. Data Used in Examples

Case	Descriptor Format
A	(10,10,10,10,10,10,10)
B	(10,10,10,10,50,50,50)
C	(10,10,10,10,100,100,100)
D	(5,5,5,5,5,5,5)
E	(8,8,8,8,8,8,8)

Number of records	1,440,000
Blocking factors	
Data	24
Index	128
Total descriptors	
A – D	60,469
E	16,512
Minimum data file size	40,320 Kb

Table 7.3 shows the storage overhead incurred by each method. It should be noted that this is the overhead due to the index and any wasted storage in the data level. Since cases A through D are built using algorithm *BU*, all the data blocks (except possibly the last) will be completely full and the storage overhead is due entirely to the index. Case E on the other hand will generate partially filled blocks and hence will have some waste in the data level. We can estimate the overhead due to unused space in the data level as follows.

From lemma 5.1 we can infer that all m_1 level 1 regions (and hence, all level 2 regions) will be represented by clusters in the space. Each level 1 region will have content given approximately by $1,440,000/m_1 = 88$ data records. To be consistent with cases A–D, we will assume that each cluster is represented by a chain of blocks. Since the data blocking factor is 24, it will take $88/24 \approx 4$ blocks on average to store a cluster and hence, $4(16,384) = 65,536$ blocks to store the entire file. In cases A–D the data file is fully packed and stored in 60,000 blocks, so case E incurs a 5,536 block overhead in the data level. Using the minimal record size of 28 bits, this works out to 3,720.19Kb of absolute overhead. The overhead due to the index is 924.67Kb for a total storage cost of 4,644.86Kb as shown in table 7.3.

This storage overhead in the data level can be reduced considerably by a variety of intelligent allocation strategies. Specifically, a variable block length would be

Table 7.3. Storage Overhead

	A	B	C	D	E
Width	70	190	340	35	56
Overhead (Kb)	4232.83	11489.11	20559.46	2116.42	4644.86
SO	.11	.29	.51	.05	.12

Table 7.4. Retrieval Performance

Number Attributes	Number Queries	Expected Accesses				
		A	B	C	D	E
1	7	22568.5	11963.8	8709.8	14951.0	15056.4
2	21	7063.6	2298.0	1338.1	3669.6	3780.8
3	35	1791.0	460.0	257.3	908.2	954.0
4	35	399.7	107.1	70.5	230.7	243.2
5	21	85.1	29.5	23.5	61.2	63.6
6	7	18.4	8.8	7.9	17.4	17.6
7	1	4.5	3.0	2.9	5.6	5.7
	$E1$	3030.8	1201.1	796.0	1755.8	1796.5

Table 7.5. Performance Comparison

	A	B	C	D	E
SO / SO_A	1.00	2.71	4.86	.50	1.10
$E1 / E1_A$	1.00	.40	.26	.58	.59

appropriate for storing clusters. This could be implemented in many ways. One interesting approach is the frame memory of March, Severance and Wilens (1981). The interested reader is referred to their paper for the details of this storage architecture.

Even using small chained blocks to store the clusters, it can be seen from table 7.3 that case E has a reasonable storage cost. It is comparable to case A and superior to cases B and C. Only case D uses less storage.

The retrieval performance of these methods is shown in table 7.4. The worst case match probabilities of equation (7.8) were used to generate the performance data for case E. This gives $\rho_{1j} = 0.25$ and $\rho_{2j} = 0.5$ for the field match probabilities at levels 1 and 2 respectively. In addition, the number of data block accesses per cluster was assumed to be $88/24 = 3.66$ on average.

The retrieval performance of the file constructed by algorithm *DCC* is comparable to that of case D. Although this represents an improvement over case A, it is not as good as cases B and C. This is to be expected since we are using a fairly coarse partition for case E. (It is possible to improve the performance of algorithm *DCC* considerably by refining the partition.) These comparisons are summarized in table 7.5.

There is an interesting way in which the storage overhead and potentially the performance of algorithm *DCC* can be improved. Earlier in this section we observed that the behavior of the cluster descriptors led to an opportunity for reducing the storage requirement of the index generated by algorithm *DCC*. Since the cluster descriptors can be expected to have all b_{ij} bits set, we can develop an index compression scheme by considering the clusters and their defining regions to be equivalent. The following informal discussion and example will serve to illustrate this technique.

Consider a descriptor at level i. If we assume that field j has all b_{ij} bits set, an equivalent descriptor can be formed by replacing each contiguous set of b_{ij} zeros by one zero and the b_{ij} ones by a single one. The new descriptor will have m_{ij} bits set in field j. After all the fields have been reduced in this manner, the new descriptor will have width $w' = \Sigma m_{ij}$. This process can be regarded as a homomorphic contraction (Pfaltz 1977) of the original space into a space of lower resolution. Notice that this compression scheme will guarantee the worst case behavior of the retrieval algorithm. But, as the example above illustrates, this performance is reasonable and can be improved by using a finer partition. Figure 7.4 illustrates how this compression scheme can be applied to the two-dimensional example of figure 7.3. The figure shows how the lower left quadrant would be compressed.

The savings in index storage can be considerable. In the case of the earlier example the level 1 descriptors can be reduced to 4-bit fields and the level 2 descriptors to 2-bit fields. The overhead of the index would then be

$$(16,384)(28) + (128)(14) = 460.5\text{Kb},$$

Figure 7.4. Example of Index File Compression

	Original Index	Compressed Index
Level 0:	00110000 00110000	0100 0100
	00110000 11000000	0100 1000
	11000000 00110000	1000 0100
	11000000 11000000	1000 1000
		1100 1100
Level 1:	11110000 11110000	10 10

which is approximately a 50 percent reduction in the storage overhead due to the index. This reduction in overhead is also achieved with no reduction in retrieval performance.

While this reduction in index overhead is significant, its greatest potential is to improve retrieval performance. If the index can be compressed so that most or all of it can reside in main memory, the increase in retrieval efficiency will be substantial. In this case, the expected number of accesses will be confined to data blocks with all index activity occurring in faster main memory.

We observed at the outset of this section that algorithm *DCC* was similar to the MDD of Liou and Yao differing chiefly in the structure of the index. To review, this method partitions each attribute domain V_j into m_j approximately equal pieces ($|V_j|/m_j$). Records are placed in buckets corresponding to subregions of the space and a directory of the subregions is maintained. We will conclude this section with a continuation of the preceding example where we now compare the performance of algorithm *DCC* with MDD.

The total space required to store the MDD is given by Liou and Yao as

$$S(0) = \sum_{k=1}^{f} L_k \prod_{j=k}^{f} m_j + LP \sum_{j=1}^{f} m_j, \qquad (7.9)$$

where L_k denotes the size or length of attribute k, m_j is the number of pieces that the domain of attribute j is partitioned into, and LP is the size of a pointer.

The expected number of page (block) accesses needed to satisfy a query Q is given by

$$\frac{S(0)}{PAGESIZE} + \frac{\prod_{i=1}^{f} m_i}{\prod_{j \in Q} m_j} \qquad (7.10)$$

The first term in (7.10) represents the number of page accesses necessary to fetch and search the entire MDD. The second term is the number of data pages accessed.

Although Liou and Yao point out that a multilevel MDD could be formed by creating a second level MDD indexing the first, they gave no indication of how this would be accomplished or how the performance would be affected. Therefore, in the following example we will assume (as Liou and Yao did) that the entire MDD is searched to satisfy a query.

Consider again the example of retrieval performance for the 1.44M record file described in table 7.2. The construction of a MDD begins by selecting the number of pieces, m_j, into which each attribute domain is to be divided. The method used to select the m_j described by Liou and Yao considers the total number of buckets and the frequency of occurrence of each anticipated query. The idea is to make m_j proportional to the frequency of occurrence of attribute j in the anticipated queries subject to the constraint on the number of buckets, $\Pi \, m_j$. Recall in the example that the level 1 index of algorithm *DCC* partitioned the space into 16,384 regions. We will therefore choose 16,384 as the number of buckets for MDD. Without going into further detail, the process described by Liou and Yao for selecting the m_j will set $m_j = 4, j = 1,2, \ldots ,7$ in this example. This is because we assume that all queries are equally likely and $\Pi \, m_j = 4^7 = 16,384$. Again we will assume a chained bucket representation using blocks of 24 records each.

Since the descriptor format for algorithm *DCC* is seven 8-bit fields, we will assume that the attribute length is log 8 $-$ 3 bits. Further, we will assume that the size of a pointer is $\lfloor \log 1,440,000 \rfloor = 21$ bits. These assumptions are made to keep the size of the MDD as small as possible so that the influence on retrieval performance (see equation (7.10), first term) is minimized. Under these assumptions the constants in equation (7.9) are $m_j = m = 4$, $L_j = L = 3$, $j = 1,2, \ldots ,7$ and $LP = 21$.

We can now compute the size of the MDD from equation (7.9). Using the above assumptions, (7.9) simplifies to

$$S(0) = L\sum_{j=1}^{f} m^j + LP \, m^f = 3\sum_{j=1}^{7} 4^j + (21)(4^7)$$

$$= 3(21,844) + (21)(16,384) = 409.6\text{Kb}.$$

Thus, the size of the MDD is slightly smaller than the compressed index (460.5Kb) of algorithm *DCC*.

The expected retrieval performance of the MDD can be calculated directly from expression (7.10). The results of these calculations along with the data for algorithm *DCC* (see column labeled E in table 7.4) are shown in table 7.6. The MDD results are shown for three different page sizes: 1024, 2048, and 4096 bytes, respectively. Since the MDD requires 409.6Kb to store it, for these page sizes it will require 50, 25, and 13 pages respectively. Liou and Yao used a page size of 2048 bytes.

Table 7.6. IDAM (*DCC*) Compared with MDD

Expected Accesses

Number Attributes	Number Queries	IDAM DCC	MDD (1024)	MDD (2048)	MDD (4096)
1	7	15056.4	15041.4	15016.4	15004.4
2	21	3780.8	3797.8	3772.8	3760.8
3	35	954.0	987.0	962.0	950.0
4	35	243.2	284.2	259.2	247.2
5	21	63.6	108.6	83.6	71.6
6	7	17.6	64.6	39.6	27.6
7	1	5.7	53.7	28.7	16.7
	$E1$	1796.5	1829.3	1804.3	1792.3

As is characteristic of all IDAM file organizations, the retrieval performance steadily improves as more attributes are specified. Even using the largest page size, the MDD is only marginally better than algorithm *DCC* when three or fewer attributes are specified, and worse when four or more are specified.

In this example the MDD and algorithm *DCC* both make the same number of data accesses given any query. The difference in their performance results from index activity alone. They differ in the number of index accesses necessary to locate the data blocks, with algorithm *DCC* holding the edge in general. But, we reiterate, the MDD in this example is being read in its entirety for every query. This fact is responsible for a constant overhead cost for each retrieval.

Algorithm *DCC* has promise as a top-down file organization. It has good retrieval performance, low index storage overhead, and excellent insertion efficiency. In addition, it offers greater freedom and flexibility in the choice of descriptor field widths.

Algorithm *DCC* has two undesirable characteristics. The first is the possible waste of storage in the data level especially for relatively small files. However, this may be minimized by appropriate storage allocation strategies. It is further mitigated by the fact that the storage overhead will decrease as the number of records increases. This occurs because there are a fixed number of regions. When there are few records in the file, many regions will be represented by small clusters. As the file grows larger, these clusters will begin to fill up and the storage overhead will decrease. This is the same phenomenon observed by Pfaltz (1982) in connection with algorithm *CC*.

The second disadvantage is that when using a coarse partition, algorithm *DCC* will require the same number of accesses to determine that a record is not in the file as it would require if the record were there. Thus, one of the chief advantages of IDAM organizations, the power to screen out records quickly, can be compromised by a poor choice of partitions at each level. More work needs to be done in this area to determine the best partition with respect to performance for a given set of file characteristics.

8

Future Research

8.1 Summary

This book investigated a family of multi-attribute file organizations called IDAM files. Given a query Q, the IDAM techniques use an encoded index to screen data records for possible candidates satisfying Q.

Retrieval techniques based on superimposed coding use an encoded bit string as a surrogate descriptor for the data records. These descriptors are used to screen the data records during the retrieval process. Although they date back to early card filing systems, these methods form the basic technology upon which the IDAM technique is built.

A model, the D-tree, for the organization of descriptors into index files was presented. A D-tree can be implemented as a set of blocked sequential files or as a linked structure with a small storage penalty.

The term IDAM as used in this book is generic, that is, an umbrella term embracing multi-attribute file organizations that employ a D-tree index over the data file. These IDAM files are further broken into two broad classes, characterized by the insertion technique used, bottom-up or top-down. The principal difference in these insertion philosophies results from the role the index plays during insertion. In the bottom-up methods, a newly inserted record is first placed in the data file and then the index is updated accordingly. In the top-down methods, the D-tree is examined to help find the "best" location in which to store the data record. This approach attempts to cluster like data records into physically adjacent locations.

The ordinary file operations on IDAM files are straightforward and present only minor implementation difficulties. The chief difficulties arise in the maintenance of the index which must ensure that a complete index remains complete after a transaction has been applied. The operation of IDAM files in a concurrent environment is facilitated by simple algorithms for implementing a variant of the predicate locks of Eswaran et al. (1976).

Much of this book concentrated on the analysis of particular IDAM file organizations. In chapter 4 the work of Pfaltz, et al. (1980) on the expected number of accesses needed to satisfy a query was reviewed and extended. The concept of a randomly organized file was introduced and analyzed to determine retrieval performance. This organization was shown to be suitable for small files since a potentially large storage penalty is exacted to maintain a desired level of retrieval performance.

In chapter 5, IDAM files were investigated when the descriptors are sorted. It was shown that this results in a fairly unbalanced retrieval structure; that is, some queries are answered very efficiently at the expense of others which have extremely poor response. The main result of this investigation was the observation that retrieval performance is affected by the size of the conceptual bucket space into which the records are placed. When the number of records in the file is small with respect to the bucket space, good retrieval performance can be achieved, but a large storage penalty is incurred. On the other hand, when the number of data records is large with respect to the bucket space, a more balanced retrieval structure with low storage overhead results.

In chapter 6, the performance metrics for storage overhead and retrieval performance used in this book were presented. The behavior of sorted IDAM files was examined and empirical comparisons of retrieval behavior and storage overhead were presented for sorted IDAM files and inverted files. The sorted IDAM files exhibited better performance in general than did the equivalent inverted file systems. In addition, for the files examined, the sorted IDAM files required approximately one tenth of the space used by the inverted files.

The bottom-up methods analyzed in chapter 4 and 5 were found to be quite restrictive with respect to the choice of various system parameters. Top-down methods which overcome these restrictions were discussed in chapter 7. In general, top-down methods exhibit better retrieval performance, but involve more storage overhead than bottom-up methods. Several heuristic approaches were discussed and their relationship to bottom-up methods was identified.

A particular clustering heuristic, algorithm *DCC*, emerged as a promising general approach to IDAM file organizations for very large files. This method constructs very compact *D*-trees with good retrieval performance and which are easy to maintain. A disadvantage seems to be a potential for some storage overhead in the data level.

In summary, the *D*-tree is a simple unifying concept for storage and retrieval methods based on superimposed coded indexes. The IDAM file is based on a *D*-tree index into a data file. IDAM files are promising as multi-attribute file organizations because:

1. They are easy to implement and maintain.
2. The data file and index file(s) can be considered logically separate and may be physically separate.
3. The same retrieval software may be used for various tree construction philosophies.
4. A large class of query types is supportable.
5. Sequential access is efficient.

6. Concurrent access is easy and flexible. IDAM files offer the potential to implement predicate locks (Eswaran et al. 1976) efficiently.
7. Most algorithms are simple enough to be implemented easily in hardware. Or for example, a continuously running channel program can search the index as has been done for ISAM files on the IBM System/370 (Bradley 1982).

Several tools were developed for conducting the research underlying this book. Two IDAM file systems running under UNIX were implemented. One is a straightforward bottom-up system. The other is a generalized heuristic top-down system employing a bounded breadth first search (BBFS) to implement the heuristics. This system is quite flexible and the BBFS can be varied from greedy to exhaustive by the specification of cost functions describing the desired heuristic.

Both systems were coded in the *C* programming language (Kernighan and Ritchie 1978). By way of crude comparison of the two methods, the bottom-up system required 1,383 lines of code and used approximately 23.5K bytes of memory; the top-down system required 1,778 lines of code and 25.5K bytes of memory. The main difference in the two implementations is the insertion routine requiring 88 and 483 lines of code respectively. It should be noted that these figures are somewhat inflated since the implementations were research tools and not production systems. Therefore, they contain excess code used to instrument and monitor the system. In any case, this is still a small file support system with fewer than 2,500 lines of code including file dump utilities, data record generators, and programs to gather static information.

8.2 Areas for Future Research

The results presented in this book tend to discount the value of bottom-up methods as general techniques for multi-attribute retrieval when using very large files. The top-down method of algorithm *DCC* emerged as a promising candidate in this regard. This clustering approach has potential, but is in need of further study.

We demonstrated this algorithm using a very simple partition/aggregation technique based on the presupposition that the partitioning intervals had already been selected. This is an area that needs further investigation to determine appropriate partitions given specific file characteristics. Some of the work of Liou and Yao (1977) and more recently Aho and Ullman (1979) can be applied to this partitioning problem.

An open question is: How does one construct hierarchical index files, given an arbitrary partition? Only when this question is answered can one fully exploit the potential of this technique. It will then be possible to ask: How does one construct an optimal index using algorithm *DCC*? Indeed, there may be no answer to this question, or many, depending on how one defines optimal.

Another question related to algorithm *DCC* concerns the storage of data records. A naive approach can result in a waste of secondary storage. This may be mitigated somewhat by newer memory management architectures (e.g., the frame memory of March, Severance and Wilens [1981]), but has the potential to be a troublesome implementation issue. The full potential of algorithm *DCC* will only be realized when these issues have been resolved.

Finally, one of the drawbacks of the IDAM file organization lies in its inherent flexibility; an encoding method must be supplied by a user as part of the file specification. Further research is needed in this area if the user is to be relieved of this burden.

In a different vein, one goal of this book was to compare and contrast the IDAM file organization with comparable multi-attribute file organizations. In many ways, this was the most troublesome aspect of the research. There do not seem to be any accepted standards in the literature for comparisons of this sort. Some authors stop at complexity analysis. While this is theoretically important, it does not give the practitioner any real feel for behavior. Others are content to select "representative" data sets and report the observed performance for these hypothetical situations. This approach has more intuitive appeal, but is subject to the attack that the data is biased or does not necessarily represent the behavior fairly. Finally, the most common approach is a qualitative discussion of the relative merits of a file organization given various anticipated real situations. This is fairly informative, but offers no quantitative performance results.

Compounding the difficulties inherent in comparing file organizations is the fact that there is no general agreement on the unit of performance. Complexity results are usually stated as functions of N, the number of data records. Illustrative examples are generally concerned with the number of secondary storage accesses or the number of buckets referenced. There are subtle differences in these measures which are greatly influenced by storage techniques. For the IDAM file we have deliberately chosen the most pessimistic measure where we equate the number of secondary storage accesses with the number of blocks accessed. This will generally be true for the data file, but the index can be organized to reduce this number considerably. It seems clear that this is an area which would benefit from increased research.

Finally, we have made no attempt to create optimal organizations, preferring instead to create a framework in which these methods can be studied. It does not seem appropriate to attempt to optimize a phenomenon until its properties are well understood. It is hoped that this book has made a contribution in this area and will be useful to other researchers interested in this problem.

Appendix A

Corollary 4.4.1: Let X be the discrete random variable with pmf given by

$$s(t) = \frac{C_t^k \, S_t^j \, t!}{w^t} \; .$$

X has mean and variance given by

(a) $\quad \mu(w,r) = w \left[1 - \left| 1 - \frac{1}{w} \right|^r \right]$

(b) $\quad \sigma^2(w,r) = w \left| \frac{w-1}{w} \right|^r + w\,(w-1) \left| \frac{w-2}{w} \right|^r - w^2 \left| \frac{w-1}{w} \right|^{2r}$

$$= \left| w - \mu(w,r) \right| \left| \mu(w,r) - \mu(w-1,r) \right|$$

Proof:

The mean and variance of the random variable X can be found from the moment generating function

$$M(t) = \frac{e^{wt}}{w^t} \sum_{k=0}^{w} C_k^w \, (w-k)^r \left[\frac{1}{e^t} - 1 \right]^k$$

of theorem 4.4. This can be rewritten as

$$M(t) = \frac{1}{w^t} \sum_{k=0}^{w} C_k^w \, (w-k)^r \, e^{wt} \, (e^{-t} - 1)^k \; .$$

Part (a):

The mean of the distribution is given by $\mu(w,r) = M'(0)$. Let

$$\delta(k,t) = e^{wt}(e^{-t}-1)^k .$$

Then

$$M'(t) = \frac{1}{w^r} \sum_{k=0}^{w} C_k^w (w-k)^r \, \delta'(k,t) .$$

The first derivative of $\delta(k,t)$ with respect to t is

$$\delta'(k,t) = we^{wt}(e^{-t}-1)^k - ke^{(w-1)t}(e^{-t}-1)^{k-1} .$$

Thus,

$$M'(t) = \frac{1}{w^r} \left\{ C_0^w \, w^r \, (we^{wt}) + C_1^w \, (w-1)^r \left[we^{wt}(e^{-t}-1) - e^{(w-1)t} \right] \right.$$
$$\left. + \sum_{k=2}^{w} C_k^w \, (w-k)^r \, \delta'(k,t) \right\} .$$

Since both terms of $\delta'(k,t)$ contain a positive power of $(e^{-t}-1)$ for $k \geq 2$, it follows that all the terms in the last sum vanish at $t=0$. Hence,

$$\mu(w,r) = M'(0) = \frac{1}{w^r} \left[w^{r+1} - w(w-1)^r \right]$$

$$= w - w \left[\frac{w-1}{w} \right]^r \;\; = \;\; w \left[1 - \left[1 - \frac{1}{w} \right]^r \right]$$

Part (b):

The variance of the distribution is given by

$$\sigma^2(w,r) = M''(0) - \mu(w,r)^2 .$$

Taking the second derivative of the moment generating function with respect to t yields

$$M''(t) = \frac{1}{w^r} \sum_{k=0}^{w} C_k^w (w-k)^r \, \delta''(k,t) .$$

The second derivative of $\delta(k,t)$ with respect to t is

$$\delta''(k,t) = w^2 e^{wt}(e^{-t}-1)^k - kwe^{(w-1)t}(e^{-t}-1)^{k-1}$$

$$- k(w-1)e^{(w-1)t}(e^{-t}-1)^{k-1}$$

$$+ k(k-1)e^{(w-2)t}(e^{-t}-1)^{k-2}$$

$$= w^2 e^{wt}(e^{-t}-1)^k - k(2w-1)e^{(w-1)t}(e^{-t}-1)^{k-1}$$

$$+ k(k-1)e^{(w-2)t}(e^{-t}-1)^{k-2}$$

Evaluating $\delta''(k,t)$ for $0 \leqslant k \leqslant 2$ yields

$$\delta''(0,t) = w^2 e^{wt}$$

$$\delta''(1,t) = w^2 e^{wt}(e^{-t}-1) - (2w-1)e^{(w-1)t}$$

$$\delta''(2,t) = w^2 e^{wt}(e^{-t}-1)^2 - 2(2w-1)e^{(w-1)t}(e^{-t}-1) + 2e^{(w-2)t}$$

Since $\delta''(k,0)=0$ for $k \geqslant 3$, we have

$$M''(0) = \frac{1}{w^r}\left\{C_0^w\, w^r\, \delta''(0,0) + C_1^w\,(w-1)^r\,\delta''(1,0) + C_2^w\,(w-2)^r\,\delta''(2,0)\right\}$$

$$= \frac{1}{w^r}\left\{C_0^w\, w^r\,(w^2) + C_1^w\,(w-1)^r\,(-(2w-1)) + C_2^w\,(w-2)^r\,(2)\right\}$$

$$= \frac{1}{w^r}\left\{w^{r+2} - w(w-1)^r(2w-1) + w(w-1)(w-2)^r\right\}$$

$$= w^2 - w(2w-1)\left|\frac{w-1}{w}\right|^r + w(w-1)\left|\frac{w-2}{w}\right|^r .$$

The square of the mean is from part (a):

$$\mu(w,r)^2 = w^2 \left| 1 - \left| \frac{w-1}{w} \right|^r \right|^2$$

$$= w^2 \left\{ 1 - 2 \left| \frac{w-1}{w} \right|^r + \left| \frac{w-1}{w} \right|^{2r} \right\}.$$

Now the variance can be evaluated directly.

$$\sigma^2(w,r) = M''(0) - \mu(w,r)^2$$

$$= w^2 - w(2w-1)\left| \frac{w-1}{w} \right|^r + w(w-1)\left| \frac{w-2}{w} \right|^r$$

$$- w^2 + 2w^2 \left| \frac{w-1}{w} \right|^r - w^2 \left| \frac{w-1}{w} \right|^{2r}$$

$$= w \left| \frac{w-1}{w} \right|^r + w(w-1)\left| \frac{w-2}{w} \right|^r - w^2 \left| \frac{w-1}{w} \right|^{2r}$$

The recurrence relation in part (b) results from a straightforward algebraic manipulation of the expression given for the variance. It may be easily verified by substituting the expression given for the mean in part (a). For further details see the derivation of equation (B.16) in Appendix B.

Corollary 4.4.2: The asymptotic behavior of the expressions given in corollary 4.4.1 for the mean and variance of the discrete random variable X can be characterized as follows.

(a) $\lim_{r \to \infty} \mu(w,r) = w$ (d) $\lim_{r \to \infty} \sigma^2(w,r) = 0$

(b) $\lim_{w \to \infty} \mu(w,r) = r$ (e) $\lim_{w \to \infty} \sigma^2(w,r) = 0$

(c) $\mu(w,1) = \mu(1,r) = 1$ (f) $\sigma^2(w,1) = \sigma^2(1,r) = 0$

Proof:

Recall from corollary 4.4.1(a) that the mean of the random variable X is given by:

$$\mu(w,r) = w\left[1 - \left[\frac{w-1}{w}\right]^r\right].$$

Parts (a) and (c) follow by inspection.

Part (b):

$$\lim_{w \to \infty} \mu(w,r) = \lim_{w \to \infty} w\left[1 - \left[\frac{w-1}{w}\right]^r\right]$$

$$= \lim_{w \to \infty} \frac{1 - \left[\frac{w-1}{w}\right]^r}{\frac{1}{w}}$$

Applying l'Hopital's rule yields

$$\lim_{w \to \infty} \mu(w,r) = \lim_{w \to \infty} r\left[1 - \frac{1}{w}\right]^{r-1}$$

$$= r$$

From corollary 4.4.1(b), the variance of the random variable X is

$$\sigma^2(w,r) = w\left[\frac{w-1}{w}\right]^r + w(w-1)\left[\frac{w-2}{w}\right]^r - w^2\left[\frac{w-1}{w}\right]^{2r}.$$

Part (d) follows immediately.

Part (e):

As an intuitive argument for (e), note that as w grows without bound, the factors in parenthesis all approach 1. Thus,

$$\lim_{w \to \infty} \sigma^2(w,r) \to w + w(w-1) - w^2 = 0.$$

More formally,

$$\sigma^2(w,r) = w\left|\frac{w-1}{w}\right|^r + w(w-1)\left|\frac{w-2}{w}\right|^r - w^2\left|\frac{w-1}{w}\right|^{2r}$$

$$w^{2r}\sigma^2(w,r) = w^{r+1}(w-1)^r + w^{r+1}(w-1)(w-2)^r - w^2(w-1)^{2r}$$

$$= w^{r+1}\left[(w-1)^r + (w-1)(w-2)^r\right] - w^2(w-1)^{2r} \tag{A.1}$$

Expanding the first term on the right hand side of equation A.1 yields:

$$w^{r+1}\left[(w-1)^r + (w-1)(w-2)^r\right]$$

$$= w^{r+1}\left\{w^r - rw^{r-1} + O\left[w^{r-2}\right]\right.$$

$$\left. + (w-1)\left[w^r - 2rw^{r-1} + 2r(r-1)w^{r-2} - O\left[w^{r-3}\right]\right]\right\}$$

$$= w^{r+1}\left\{w^r - rw^{r-1} + O\left[w^{r-2}\right] + w^{r+1} - 2rw^r + 2r(r-1)w^{r-1} + O\left[w^{r-2}\right]\right.$$

$$\left. - w^r + 2rw^{r-1} - 2r(r-1)w^{r-2} - O\left[w^{r-3}\right]\right\}$$

$$= w^{r+1}\left\{w^{r+1} - 2rw^r + \left[2r - r + 2r(r-1)\right]w^{r-1} + O\left[w^{r-2}\right]\right\}$$

$$= w^{r+1}\left\{w^{r+1} - 2rw^r + r(2r-1)w^{r-1} + O\left[w^{r-2}\right]\right\}$$

$$= w^{2r+2} - 2rw^{2r+1} + r(2r-1)w^{2r} + O\left[w^{2r-1}\right] \tag{A.2}$$

Applying the binomial theorem to the second term on the right hand side of equation A.1 yields:

$$w^2(w-1)^{2r} = w^2\left[w^{2r} - 2rw^{2r-1} + r(2r-1)w^{2r-2} - O\left|w^{2r-3}\right|\right]$$

$$= w^{2r+2} - 2rw^{2r+1} + r(2r-1)w^{2r} - O\left|w^{2r-1}\right| \qquad (A.3)$$

Substituting equations A.2 and A.3 back into equation A.1 yields

$$w^{2r}\sigma^2(w,r) = O\left|w^{2r-1}\right|$$

which implies that $\sigma^2(w,r) = O(1/w)$. The result now follows directly.

Part (f):

$$\sigma^2(w,1) = (w-1) + (w-1)(w-2) - (w-1)^2$$

$$= (w-1)[1 + w - 2 - w + 1] = 0$$

This concludes the proof of the corollary. $\square$

Appendix B

Consider a superimposed code word composed of r width w weight k random binary code words **OR**-ed together. Let $\phi(t)$ be the probability that the superimposed code word is of weight t. Roberts [ROBE79] has shown that

$$\phi(t) = (-1)^t C_t^w \sum_{j=0}^{t} (-1)^j C_j^t [C_k^j / C_k^w]^r \ . \tag{B.1}$$

Let $p = \text{Pr}\{$ any single bit position has the value 1 $\}$ then

$$p = 1 - \left[1 - \frac{k}{w}\right]^r \ .$$

The mean weight of the superimposed code word is given by

$$\bar{b} = \sum_{t=0}^{w} t \ \phi(t)$$

$$= w \left[1 - (C_k^{w-1} / C_k^w)^r\right] \tag{B.2}$$

$$= w \left[1 - \left[1 - \frac{k}{w}\right]^r\right]$$

$$= wp$$

We now extend Roberts' work by deriving the variance of the weight distribution. To begin we will calculate the second moment, m_2, of the distribution. From the definition of the second moment and equation B.1 we have

$$m_2 = \sum_{t=0}^{w} t^2 \phi(t) = \sum_{t=0}^{w} t^2 \left\{ (-1)^y \, C_t^w \sum_{j=0}^{t} (-1)^j \, C_j^t [C_k^j / C_k^w]^y \right\} .$$

Changing the order of summation and rearranging yields

$$m_2 = \sum_{j=0}^{w} (-1)^j [C_k^j / C_k^w]^y \sum_{t=0}^{w} (-1)^y \, t^2 C_t^w C_j^t \tag{B.3}$$

since $C_j^t = 0$ for $t < j$. To evaluate the second sum in this expression we need to eliminate the t^2 factor.

Claim:

$$t^2 C_t^w = w^2 C_{t-1}^{w-1} - w(w-1) C_{t-1}^{w-2} . \tag{B.4}$$

Proof:

$$t^2 C_t^w = (tw - tw + t^2) C_t^w = tw \, C_t^w - t(w-t) C_t^w$$

$$= tw \, \frac{w!}{t!(w-t)!} - t(w-t) \frac{w!}{t!(w-t)!}$$

$$= w^2 \frac{(w-1)!}{(t-1)!(w-t)!} - w(w-1) \frac{(w-2)!}{(t-1)!(w-t-1)!}$$

$$= w^2 C_{t-1}^{w-1} - w(w-1) C_{t-1}^{w-2} \qquad \square$$

Substituting equation B.4 into the second sum of equation B.3 yields

$$\sum_{t=0}^{w} (-1)^y \, t^2 C_t^w C_j^t = \sum_{t=0}^{w} (-1)^y \left\{ w^2 C_{t-1}^{w-1} - w(w-1) C_{t-1}^{w-2} \right\} C_j^t$$

$$= w^2 \sum_{t=0}^{w} (-1)^y \, C_{t-1}^{w-1} C_j^t - w(w-1) \sum_{t=0}^{w} (-1)^y \, C_{t-1}^{w-2} C_j^t \tag{B.5}$$

The sums in B.5 can now be evaluated using the identity [KNUT73a]

$$\sum_k C_k^r C_n^{s+k} (-1)^k = (-1)^r C_{n-r}^s , \quad r \geqslant 0 . \tag{B.6}$$

Rewriting the first sum in B.5 as

$$\sum_{t=0}^{w} (-1)^t C_{t-1}^{w-1} C_j^t = - \sum_{t=0}^{w} (-1)^{t-1} C_{t-1}^{w-1} C_j^t$$

and letting $r = w - 1, k = t - 1, s = 1$ and $n = j$ in B.6 yields

$$\sum_{t=0}^{w} (-1)^t C_{t-1}^{w-1} C_j^t = -(-1)^{w-1} C_{j-w+1}^1$$

$$= (-1)^w C_{j-w+1}^1 \tag{B.7}$$

Note $j \leqslant w$ and

$$C_{j-w+1}^1 = \begin{cases} 0, & j < w-1 \\ 1, & j \geqslant w-1 \end{cases}$$

Rewriting the second sum in B.5 and letting $r = w - 2, k = t - 1, s = 1$ and $n = j$ in B.6

yields

$$\sum_{t=0}^{w} (-1)^t C_{t-1}^{w-2} C_j^t = - \sum_{t=0}^{w} (-1)^{t-1} C_{t-1}^{w-2} C_j^t$$

$$= -(-1)^{w-2} C_{j-w+2}^1$$

$$= -(-1)^w C_{j-w+2}^1 \tag{B.8}$$

Again note $j \leqslant w$ and

$$C_{j-w+2}^1 = \begin{cases} 0, & j < w-2, \text{ and } j = w \\ 1, & j \geqslant w-1 \end{cases}$$

Substituting B.7 and B.8 back into B.5 we get

$$\sum_{t=0}^{w} (-1)^t t^2 C_t^w C_j^t = w^2 [(-1)^w C_{j-w+1}^1] - w(w-1)[-(-1)^w C_{j-w+2}^1]$$

$$= (-1)^w [w^2 C_{j-w+1}^1 + w(w-1) C_{j-w+2}^1] \tag{B.9}$$

We can now substitute B.9 for the second sum in B.3 to get

$$m_2 = \sum_{j=0}^{w} (-1)^j [C_j^j / C_k^w]^r \left\{ (-1)^w [w^2 C_{j-w+1}^1 + w(w-1)C_{j-w+2}^1] \right\}$$

The range of the summation can be changed to $w-2 \leqslant j \leqslant w$ (see notes to equations B.7 and B.8) and the sum reduced to three terms as follows.

$$m_2 = \sum_{j=w-2}^{w} (-1)^{w+j} [C_j^j / C_k^w]^r [w^2 C_{j-w+1}^1 + w(w-1)C_{j-w+2}^1]$$

$$= (-1)^{2w-2} [C_k^{w-2}/C_k^w]^r [w^2 C_{-1}^1 + w(w-1)C_0^1]$$

$$+ (-1)^{2w-1} [C_k^{w-1}/C_k^w]^r [w^2 C_0^1 + w(w-1)C_1^1]$$

$$+ (-1)^{2w} [C_k^w / C_k^w]^r [w^2 C_1^1 + w(w-1)C_2^1]$$

$$= w(w-1)[C_k^{w-2}/C_k^w]^r - (w^2 + w(w-1))[C_k^{w-1}/C_k^w]^r + w^2$$

$$= w(w-1)[C_k^{w-2}/C_k^w]^r - (2w^2 - w)[C_k^{w-1}/C_k^w]^r + w^2$$

$$= w(w-1)[C_k^{w-2}/C_k^w]^r + w[C_k^{w-1}/C_k^w]^r$$

$$- 2w^2[C_k^{w-1}/C_k^w]^r + w^2 \tag{B.10}$$

Let V denote the variance of the weight distribution, then $V = m_2 - \bar{b}^2$. Recall from B.2 that

$$\bar{b} = w(1 - [C_i^{w-1}/C_k^w]^r)$$

and hence,

$$\bar{b}^2 = w^2(1 - 2[C_i^{w-1}/C_k^w]^r + [C_k^{w-1}/C_k^w]^{2r})$$

$$= w^2 - 2w^2[C_k^{w-1}/C_k^w]^r + w^2[C_k^{w-1}/C_k^w]^{2r} \tag{B.11}$$

Subtracting B.11 from B.10 we get for the variance

$$V = w(w-1)[C_k^{w-2}/C_k^w]^r + w[C_k^{w-1}/C_k^w]^r - w^2[C_k^{w-1}/C_k^w]^{2r} \tag{B.12}$$

To remove the binomial coefficients from equation B.12 note that

$$C_k^{w-1} = \frac{(w-1)!}{k!(w-k-1)!} = \frac{w-1}{w-k-1} \frac{(w-2)!}{k!(w-k-2)!}$$

$$= \frac{w-1}{w-k-1} C_k^{w-2} \tag{B.13}$$

and further

$$C_k^{w-1}/C_k^w = \frac{(w-1)!}{k!(w-k-1)!} \frac{k!(w-k)!}{w!} = \frac{w-k}{w} \tag{B.14}$$

We can now use B.13 and B.14 to simplify equation B.12 as follows.

$$V = w(w-1)\left|\frac{w-k-1}{w-1}\right|^r [C_k^{w-1}/C_k^w]^r + w[C_k^{w-1}/C_k^w]^r - w^2[C_k^{w-1}/C_k^w]^{2r}$$

$$= w(w-1)\left|\frac{w-k-1}{w-1}\right|^r \left|\frac{w-k}{w}\right|^r + w\left|\frac{w-k}{w}\right|^r - w^2\left|\frac{w-k}{w}\right|^{2r}$$

$$= w(w-1)\left|\frac{(w-k)(w-k-1)}{w(w-1)}\right|^r + w\left|\frac{w-k}{w}\right|^r - w^2\left|\frac{w-k}{w}\right|^{2r} \tag{B.15}$$

Equation B.15 can also be expressed as a recurrence relation. We begin by rewriting B.15 as follows.

$$V = w\left|\frac{w-k}{w}\right|^r \left\{(w-1)\left|\frac{w-k-1}{w-1}\right|^r + 1 - w\left|\frac{w-k}{w}\right|^r\right\}$$

$$= w\left|\frac{w-k}{w}\right|^r \left\{w - w\left|\frac{w-k}{w}\right|^r - w + 1 - (w-1)\left|\frac{w-k-1}{w-1}\right|^r\right\}$$

$$= (w-\bar{b})\left\{\bar{b} - (w-1)\left|1 - \left|\frac{w-k-1}{w-1}\right|^r\right|\right\}$$

If we show the parameters of V and $\bar{b}$ explicitly, we can rewrite this expression as the following recurrence in w

$$V(w,k,r) = \left[w - \bar{b}(w,k,r) \right] \left[\bar{b}(w,k,r) - \bar{b}(w-1,k,r) \right].$$

(B.16)

Appendix C

Recall from theorem 5.5 that

$$\bar{s}(r) = w - \left|\frac{w(1+\alpha)-2}{2\alpha}\right|\left|\frac{1+\alpha}{2}\right|^r + \left|\frac{w(1-\alpha)-2}{2\alpha}\right|\left|\frac{1-\alpha}{2}\right|^r$$

where

$$\alpha = \left|1 - 4\frac{t}{w}\right|^{1/2}.$$

To simplify the notation we have dropped the subscript j.

Corollary 5.5.1: Two special cases of theorem 5.5 are

$$(a) \quad \bar{s}(r) = 1 \qquad\qquad t = 0$$

$$(b) \quad \bar{s}(r) = w\left|1 - t^r\right| \qquad t = 1 - \frac{1}{w}$$

Again the subscripts have been omitted.

Proof:

Since $t = 0$ implies that $\alpha = 1$, part (a) follows immediately.

Part (b):

When $t = 1 - \frac{1}{w}$ we have

$$\alpha = \left|1 - \frac{4}{w}\left|1 - \frac{1}{w}\right|\right|^{1/2} = \frac{w-2}{w}.$$

Substituting for α, we have

$$\frac{w(1+\alpha)-2}{2\alpha} = w \; , \quad \left|\frac{1+\alpha}{2}\right|^r = t' \; , \quad \text{and} \quad \frac{w(1-\alpha)-2}{2\alpha} = 0$$

from which the result follows directly.

Corollary 5.5.2: Let $\bar{s}_j(r,w_j)$ denote the expression in theorem 5.5.

$$(a) \quad \lim_{r \to \infty} \bar{s}_j(r,w_j) = \begin{array}{ll} 1 & , \alpha = 1 \\ w_j & , \alpha < 1 \end{array}$$

$$(b) \quad \lim_{w_j \to \infty} \bar{s}_j(r,w_j) = 1 + (r-1)t_j$$

Proof: We will again drop the subscripts.

Part (a):

Case (1): $\alpha = 1$

Since $\alpha = 1$ implies that $t = 0$, the result follows from corollary 5.5.1(a).

Case (2): $\alpha < 1$

When $\alpha < 1$ it follows that

$$\lim_{r \to \infty}\left|\frac{1+\alpha}{2}\right|^r = 0 \quad \text{and} \quad \lim_{r \to \infty}\left|\frac{1-\alpha}{2}\right|^r = 0$$

and hence,

$$\lim_{r \to \infty}\bar{s}(r) = w \; .$$

Part (b):

$$\lim_{w \to \infty}\bar{s}(r) = \lim_{w \to \infty}\left\{ w - \left|\frac{w(1+\alpha)-2}{2\alpha}\right|\left|\frac{1+\alpha}{2}\right|^r \right\}$$

$$+ \lim_{w \to \infty}\left\{\left|\frac{w(1-\alpha)-2}{2\alpha}\right|\left|\frac{1-\alpha}{2}\right|^r\right\}$$

(C.1)

We may simplify this expression somewhat by noting that

$$\lim_{w \to \infty} \alpha = \lim_{w \to \infty} \left| 1 - 4\frac{t}{w} \right|^{\frac{1}{2}} = 1 . \tag{C.2}$$

Thus the second term in (C.1) will vanish in the limit and we can rewrite (C.1) as

$$\lim_{w \to \infty} \bar{s}(r) = \lim_{w \to \infty} \left\{ w - \left| \frac{w(1+\alpha) - 2}{2\alpha} \right| \left| \frac{1+\alpha}{2} \right|^r \right\}$$

$$= \lim_{w \to \infty} \left\{ w - w\frac{1}{\alpha} \left| \frac{1+\alpha}{2} \right|^{r+1} + \frac{1}{\alpha} \left| \frac{1+\alpha}{2} \right|^r \right\}$$

$$= \lim_{w \to \infty} \left\{ \frac{1}{\alpha} \left| \frac{1+\alpha}{2} \right|^r \right\} + \lim_{w \to \infty} \left\{ w \left| 1 - \frac{1}{\alpha} \left| \frac{1+\alpha}{2} \right|^{r+1} \right| \right\}$$

$$= 1 + \lim_{w \to \infty} \left\{ w \left| 1 - \frac{1}{\alpha} \left| \frac{1+\alpha}{2} \right|^{r+1} \right| \right\} \tag{C.3}$$

where we have again made use of (C.2) to evaluate the left hand limit.

The remaining limit in (C.3) can be evaluated using L'Hopital's rule. Thus, we have

$$\lim_{w \to \infty} \bar{s}(r) = 1 - \lim_{w \to \infty} \left\{ \frac{\dfrac{d}{dw} \left| \dfrac{1}{\alpha} \left| \dfrac{1+\alpha}{2} \right|^{r+1} \right|}{\dfrac{d}{dw} \left| \dfrac{1}{w} \right|} \right\} \tag{C.4}$$

To evaluate the derivative in the numerator of (C.4) note that

$$\frac{d}{dw} \alpha = \frac{2t}{\alpha w^2} \quad and \quad \frac{d}{dw} \left| \frac{1}{\alpha} \right| = \frac{-2t}{\alpha^3 w^2} .$$

Hence,

$$\frac{d}{dw}\left[\frac{1}{\alpha}\left(\frac{1+\alpha}{2}\right)^{r+1}\right] = \frac{(r+1)}{2\alpha}\left(\frac{1+\alpha}{2}\right)^{r}\frac{d}{dw}\alpha + \left(\frac{1+\alpha}{2}\right)^{r+1}\frac{d}{dw}\left(\frac{1}{\alpha}\right)$$

$$= \frac{(r+1)t}{\alpha^2 w^2}\left(\frac{1+\alpha}{2}\right)^{r} - \frac{2t}{\alpha^3 w^2}\left(\frac{1+\alpha}{2}\right)^{r+1}. \tag{C.5}$$

Substituting (C.5) back into (C.4) yields

$$\lim_{w\to\infty}\bar{s}(r) = 1 - \lim_{w\to\infty}\left\{-\frac{(r+1)t}{\alpha^2}\left(\frac{1+\alpha}{2}\right)^{r} + \frac{2t}{\alpha^3}\left(\frac{1+\alpha}{2}\right)^{r+1}\right\}$$

$$= 1 - [-(r+1)t + 2t]$$

$$= 1 + (r-1)t.$$

Appendix D

Derivation of an approximation to $\bar{s}(r)$:

Recall from theorem 5.5 that

$$\bar{s}(r) = w - \left|\frac{w(1+\alpha)-2}{2\alpha}\right|\left|\frac{1+\alpha}{2}\right|^r + \left|\frac{w(1-\alpha)-2}{2\alpha}\right|\left|\frac{1-\alpha}{2}\right|^r \tag{D.1}$$

where

$$\alpha = \left|1 - 4\frac{t}{w}\right|^{1/2}$$

To simplify the notation we have dropped the subscript j. When $4t/w$ is small we may approximate α and $1/\alpha$ by their Taylor series expansions. They are

$$\alpha = 1 - 2\frac{t}{w} - 2\left|\frac{t}{w}\right|^2 + O\left|\frac{t^3}{w^3}\right|$$

and

$$\frac{1}{\alpha} = 1 + 2\frac{t}{w} + 6\left|\frac{t}{w}\right|^2 + O\left|\frac{t^3}{w^3}\right| .$$

Using these expressions the following approximations to the factors in $\bar{s}(r)$ can be derived:

$$\left|\frac{w(1+\alpha)-2}{2\alpha}\right| = 1 + (w-2)\left|1 + \frac{t}{w} + 3\left|\frac{t}{w}\right|^2\right| + O\left|\frac{t^3}{w^2}\right| \tag{D.2}$$

$$\left| \frac{1+\alpha}{2} \right|^r = 1 - r\,\frac{t}{w} + O\left| \frac{t^2}{w^2} \right| \tag{D.3}$$

$$\left| \frac{w(1-\alpha)-2}{2\alpha} \right| = -1 + (w-2)\left| \frac{t}{w} + 3\left| \frac{t}{w} \right|^2 \right| + O\left| \frac{t^3}{w^2} \right| \tag{D.4}$$

$$\left| \frac{1-\alpha}{2} \right|^r = \left| \frac{t}{w} \right|^r \left| 1 + r\,\frac{t}{w} \right| + O\left| \frac{t^{r+2}}{w^{r+2}} \right| \tag{D.5}$$

It can be seen from equation (D.5) that the third term of equation (D.1) will rapidly approach zero for even small values of r. For example, equation (D.5) will have a value on the order of 10^{-5} for $\frac{t}{w} = .1$ and $r = 5$. Thus, we can get a good approximation to $\bar{s}(r)$ by substituting equations (D.2) and (D.3) into equation (D.1) and neglecting the third term. After some simplification we have

$$\bar{s}(r) = (w-1)\left| 1 + r\,\frac{t}{w} \right| - (w-2)\left| 1 + \frac{t}{w} \right| + O\left| \frac{t^2}{w^2} \right|$$

$$= \left| 1 - \frac{1}{w} \right| r\,t - \left| 1 - \frac{2}{w} \right| t + 1 + O\left| \frac{t^2}{w^2} \right|$$

$$= 1 + (r-1)\left| 1 - \frac{1}{w} \right| t + \frac{t}{w} + O\left| \frac{t^2}{w^2} \right|.$$

Bibliography

Aho, A.V., and J.D. Ullman. "Optimal Partial—Match Retrieval When Fields are Independently Specified." ACM TODS, vol. 4, no. 2 (June 1979), 168–179.

Alagar, V.S. "Algorithms for Processing Partial Match Queries Using Word Fragments." Information Systems, vol. 5, no. 4 (April 1980), 323–332.

Bentley, J.L. "Multidimensional Binary Search Trees Used for Associative Searching." CACM, vol. 18, no. 9 (September 1975), 509–517.

_____. "Multidimensional Binary Search Trees in Database Applications," IEEE Trans. Software Engineering, vol. SE-5, no. 4 (July 1979), 333–340.

_____, and J.H. Friedman. "Data Structures for Range Searching." Computing Surveys, vol. 11, no. 4 (December 1979), 397–409.

Berman, W.J., and J.L. Pfaltz. "Multi-Dimensional Bucket Arrays," Univ. of Virginia DAMACS Tech. Rpt. TR-16-78, March 78.

_____. "Use of the Indexed-Descriptor Access Method by the Federal Judicial Center." Final Report, FJC contract 17648KMN, May 1980.

Blasgen, M.W., R.G. Casey and K.P. Eswaran. "An Encoding Method for Multifield Sorting and Indexing." CACM, vol. 20, no. 11 (November 1977), 874–878.

Bloom, B.H. "Space/Time Trade-offs in Hash Coding with Allowable Errors." CACM, vol. 13, no. 7 (July 1970), 422–426.

Bolour, A. "Optimality Properties of Multiple-Key Hashing Functions." JACM, vol. 26, no. 2 (April 1979), 196–210.

Bourne, C.P. Methods of Information Handling. New York, NY: Holt, Rinehart and Winston, 1982.

Bradley, J. File and Data Base Techniques. New York, NY: Holt, Rinehart and Winston, 1982.

Burkhard, W.A. "Hashing and Trie Algorithms for Partial Match Retrieval." ACM TODS, vol 1, no. 2 (June 1976), 175–187.

_____. "Partial-Match Hash Coding: Benefits of Redundancy." ACM TODS, vol. 4, no. 2 (June 1979), 228–239.

Cagley, E.M. "A Retrieval Strategy for Large, Multi-Key Files Requiring Frequent Updating." Executive Office of the President (Office of Emergency Preparedness) TR-75, December 1971.

Cardenas, A.F. "Analysis and Performance of Inverted Data Base Structures." CACM, vol. 18, no. 5 (May 1975), 253–263.

Casey, R.G. "Design of Tree Structures for Efficient Querying." CACM, vol. 16, no. 9 (September 1973), 549–556.

Casey, R.S. and J.W. Perry, editors. Punched Cards: Their Applications to Science and Industry. New York, NY: Reinhold Publishing Corp., 1951.

Chang, C.C., R.C.T. Lee and H.C. Du. "Some Properties of Cartesian Product Files." Proc. ACM SIGMOD Conference (May 1980), 157–168.

Chang, J.M., and K.S. Fu. "A Dynamic Clustering Technique for Physical Database Design." Proc. ACM SIGMOD Conference (May 1980), 188–199.

Codd, E.F. "A Relational Model of Data for Large Shared Data Banks." CACM, vol. 13, no. 6 (June 1970), 377–387.

Coffman, E.G., and P.J. Denning. *Operating Systems Theory.* Englewood Cliffs, NJ: Prentice-Hall, 1973.

Date, C.J. *An Introduction to Database Systems.* Second edition. Reading, MA: Addison-Wesley, 1977.

Du, H.C., and J.S. Sobolewski. "Disk Allocation for Cartesian Product Files on Multiple-Disk Systems." ACM TODS, vol. 7, no. 1 (March 1982), 82–101.

Eswaran, K.P., J.N. Gray, R.A. Lorie and I.L. Traiger. "The Notions of Consistency and Predicate Locks in a Database System." CACM, vol. 19, no. 11 (November 1976), 624–633.

Files, J.R., and H.D. Huskey. "An Information Retrieval System Based on Superimposed Coding." AFIP Proc., vol. 35, 1969.

Finkel, R.A., and J.L. Bentley. "Quad Trees—A Data Structure for Retrieval on Composite Keys." Acta Informatica, vol. 4, no. 1 (1974), 1–9.

Frazer, W.D. "A Proposed System for Multiple Descriptor Data Retrieval." In *Some Problems in Information Science* (M. Kochen ed.). New York, NY: The Scarecrow Press, 1965.

French, J.C. "An Investigation of IDAM File Organizations." Ph.D. thesis, University of Virginia, 1982.

Gustafson, R.A. "A Randomized Combinatorial File Structure for Storage and Retrieval Systems." Ph.D. thesis, Univ. of South Carolina, Columbia, 1969.

Harrison, M.C. "Implementation of the Substring Test by Hashing." CACM, vol. 14, no. 12 (December 1971), 777–779.

Hsiao, D., and F. Harary. "A Formal System for Information Retrieval from Files." CACM, vol. 13, no. 2 (February 1970), 67–73.

Hutton, F.C. "PEEKABIT, Computer Offspring of Punched Card PEEKABOO, for Natural Language Searching." CACM, vol. 11, no. 9 (September 1968), 595–598.

Johnson, L.R. "An Indirect Chaining Method for Addressing on Secondary Keys." CACM, vol. 4, no. 5 (May 1961), 218–222.

Kernighan, B.W., and D.M. Ritchie. *The C Programming Language.* Englewood Cliffs, NJ: Prentice-Hall, 1978.

Knuth, D.E. *The Art of Computer Programming.* Volume 1, *Fundamental Algorithms.* (Second Edition.) Reading, MA: Addison-Wesley, 1973.

———. *The Art of Computer Programming.* Volume 3, *Searching and Sorting.* Reading, MA: Addison-Wesley, 1973.

Larson, H.J. *Introduction to Probability Theory and Statistical Inference.* Second edition. New York, NY: John Wiley & Sons, 1969.

Lee, D.T., and C.K. Wong. "Quintary Trees: A File Structure for Multidimensional Database Systems." ACM TODS, vol. 5, no. 3 (September 1980), 339–353.

Lin, W.C., R.C.T. Lee, and H.C. Du. "Common Properties of Some Multiattribute File Systems." IEEE Trans. Software Engineering, vol. SE-5, no. 2 (March 1979), 160–174.

Liou, J.H., and S.B. Yao. "Multi-dimensional Clustering for Data Base Organizations." Information Systems, vol. 2 (1977), 187–198.

Liu, C.L. *Introduction to Combinatorial Mathematics.* New York, NY: McGraw-Hill, 1968.

Lum, V.Y. "Multi-attribute Retrieval with Combined Indexes." CACM, vol. 13, no. 11 (November 1970), 660–665.

March, S., D.G. Severance and M. Wilens. "Frame Memory: A Storage Architecture to Support Rapid Design and Implementation of Efficient Databases." ACM TODS, vol. 6, no. 3 (September 1981), 441–463.

Martin, J. *Computer Data-Base Organization* Englewood Cliffs, NJ: Prentice-Hall, 1975.

Moore, R.T. "A Screening Method for Large Information Retrieval Systems." Proc. Western Joint Computer Conference, vol. 19 (1961), 259–274.

Mullin, J.K. "Retrieval—Update Speed Tradeoffs Using Combined Indices." CACM, vol. 14, no. 12 (December 1971), 775–776.

Pfaltz, J.L. *Computer Data Structures.* New York, NY: McGraw-Hill, 1977.

_____. "The Use of Indexed Descriptor Files for Retrieval in Very Large Data Bases." Batelle Contract DAAG–29–76–D–0100, October 1978.

_____. "Specifications for an Indexed Descriptor File Retrieval System." Batelle Contract DAAG–29–76–D–0100, August 1979.

_____. "Efficient Multi-Attribute Retrieval over Very Large Geographical Data Files." Proc. AUTO-CARTO IV, Washington, D.C., 1979.

_____, W.J. Berman and E.M. Cagley. "Partial-Match Retrieval Using Indexed Descriptor Files." CACM, vol. 23, no. 9 (September 1980), 522–528.

_____. "Convex Clusters in a Discrete m-Dimensional Space." Submitted to SIAM Computing, 1982.

Rivest, R. "Partial-Match Retrieval Algorithms." SIAM J. Computing, vol. 5, no. 1 (1976), 19–50.

Roberts, C.S. "Partial-Match Retrieval via the Method of Superimposed Codes." Proc. IEEE, vol. 67, no. 12 (December 1979), 1624–1642.

Rothnie, J.B., and T. Lozano. "Attribute Based File Organization in a Paged Memory Environment." CACM, vol. 17, no. 2 (February 1974), 63–69.

Schneiderman, B. "Reduced Combined Indexes for Efficient Multiple Attribute Retrieval." Information Systems, vol. 2 (1976), 149–154.

Slonim, J., L.J. MacRae, W.E. Mennie and N. Diamond. "NDX-100: An Electronic Filing Machine for the Office of the Future." IEEE Computer, vol. 14, no. 5 (May 1981), 24–36.

Vallarino, O. "On the Use of Bit Maps for Multiple Key Retrieval." ACM SIGPLAN Notices, vol. 11, special issue (March 1976), 108–114.

Wiederhold, G. *Database Design.* New York, NY: McGraw-Hill, 1977.

Wise, C.S. "Mathematical Analysis of Coding Systems." In *Punched Cards: Their Applications to Science and Industry* (R.S. Casey and J.W. Perry, editors.) New York, NY: Reinhold Publishing Corp., 1951.

Wong, E., and T.C. Chiang. "Canonical Structure in Attribute Based File Organization." CACM, vol. 14, no. 9 (September 1971), 593–597.

Yao, S.B. "Approximating Block Accesses in Database Organizations." CACM, vol. 20, no. 4 (April 1977), 260–261.

Zobrist, A.L., and F.R. Carlson, Jr. "Detection of Combined Occurrences." CACM, vol. 20, no. 1 (January 1977), 31–35.

Index